Beneath the Killing Fields

To Jack
Depth and breadth

BENEATH THE KILLING FIELDS

Exploring the Subterranean Landscapes of the Western Front

Matthew Leonard

Series Consultant:
Nicholas J. Saunders

PEN & SWORD
ARCHAEOLOGY

First published in Great Britain in 2016 by
PEN & SWORD ARCHAEOLOGY
an imprint of
Pen & Sword Books Ltd,
47 Church Street,
Barnsley,
South Yorkshire.
S70 2AS

A CIP record for this book is available from the British Library.

ISBN 978 1 78346 306 0

Printed and bound by Replika Press Pvt. Ltd.

Pen & Sword Books Ltd incorporates the Imprints of
Pen & Sword Aviation, Pen & Sword Maritime,
Pen & Sword Military, Wharncliffe Local History, Pen & Sword Select, Pen &
Sword Military Classics and Leo Cooper.

For a complete list of Pen & Sword titles please contact
Pen & Sword Books Limited
47 Church Street, Barnsley, South Yorkshire, S70 2AS, England
E-mail: enquiries@pen-and-sword.co.uk
Website: www.pen-and-sword.co.uk

Contents

Acknowledgements

First and foremost my thanks go to the Durand Group, without whom this book would not have been possible. My membership of the Group has allowed me to develop both personally and professionally, and I am indebted to all concerned for their help, knowledge and advice. In particular I would like to thank Lieutenant Colonel (Retd) Phillip Robinson and Andy Prada. Phillip is the foremost expert on the underground war in Northern France during the Great War and his attention to detail and extensive knowledge has been of great benefit to me. Andy is a founder member of the Durand Group and the project manager for our current work at Loos. For several years he has toiled tirelessly to forge links with the local community and understand the hidden secrets of the Loos battlefield. I cannot thank both of them enough for freely dedicating their time and expertise, and for being open to modern archaeological and anthropological approaches to these complex landscapes.

Professor Nicholas Saunders has assisted me with this work in too many ways to mention. Nick is the 'founding father' of modern conflict archaeology, and his open-minded approach to the study of the material culture of twentieth century conflict had a profound effect on me. This led directly to me studying for a doctorate in archaeology, and much of the research undertaken for that work is detailed in these pages. For all his help, advice and 'multi-coloured' opinions I will be forever grateful.

Writing a book is a long and often solitary experience. Through it all, my wife Kirsty has given me her full support; looking after our young child, working to support our family, accompanying me to an innumerable number of old battlefields, and allowing me the time and space to fill these pages. Without her love, friendship and encouragement I doubt this project would have been completed. Thank you for everything.

Finally, I would like to thank Pen and Sword for their patience while waiting for the finished manuscript. Both Heather and Eloise were professional, approachable and understanding as to the inevitable delays that occurred while I completed my studies. To everyone else who has contributed goes my utmost thanks and respect. I know who you are and so do you.

Glossary and Useful Terms

Bell Chamber A bell dome-like chamber that can form in a tunnel or dugout when chalk has slabbed from the sides and ceiling.

Blowing A term used to describe the detonation of a mine charge.

Camouflet An underground explosive charge primarily employed to destroy enemy tunnels. Camouflet charges do not usually break the surface.

Clay Kicking The practice of digging through clay, originally devised by sewer diggers. Clay kicking has the added advantage of being near silent and was therefore a logical adoption for tunnelling companies where the geology was relevant.

Light (Decauville) Railway Invented by Paul Decauville (1846-1922), the railway named after him consisted of narrow gauge tracks mounted to metal sleepers. It was light and manoeuvrable and used extensively during the First World War for the transport of men and equipment on the front lines.

Exteroception Outwardly orientated perception.

Face A 'face' is the front of the tunnel where the actual digging was being done, similar to a 'coal face'.

Gallery A term used to describe a tunnel, usually one that extended towards the enemy's positions.

Geophone A tool used for listening underground. Consisting of two microphones and acting in a similar way to a doctor's stethoscope. Sound waves through the ground are magnified and sounds are transmitted to each of the listener's ears, allowing a bearing to be taken on the source of the sound.

Incline A sloping entrance to a tunnel, usually from a trench and used instead of a vertical shaft. Inclines are often referred to as 'shafts' in war diaries.

Kinaesthesia The sensation of movement in the body and limbs originating in the muscles, tendons and joints.

Lateral A defensive tunnel dug parallel to the front line

	trench. Other, offensive and defensive, tunnels were then dug from the lateral. Sometimes also called a transversal.
Livens Projector	A type of mortar used primarily for delivering gas.
Mine	An explosive charge placed underground.
Pioneer Shaft	An exploratory shaft dug to connect existing features.
Proto Apparatus	Self contained breathing apparatus primarily used in mine rescue.
Proprioception	The perception of the position, state and movement of the body.
Puit	Shaft connecting the surface to a souterraine used to lift up and remove cut chalk blocks from the original quarry.
Russian Sap	A shallow tunnel or deep covered trench that could quickly have the top pulled in to expose a trench, listening post or trench mortar position.
Sap	A trench dug towards the enemy. Also sometimes used to describe a tunnel dug in a similar direction.
Seismomicrophone	An electrically powered sound detector usually linked to a central listening station responsible for a large area of front.
Sensorium	The section of the human brain tasked with the reception and interpretation of the different sensory stimulae. Also a term used to describe the human senses as a whole.
Shaft	A vertical entrance to a tunnel or dugout but often used to describe an incline.
Slabbing	Chalk is often layered in 'bedding planes' and where these are weak large sections can split apart, causing collapses.
Souterraine	A French term meaning 'underground' but often a term used to describe caves or subterranean quarries.
Stollen	A German term for a mine gallery, deep dugout or tunnel.
Subway	A communication tunnel used for the movement of troops to and from front line positions. Subways also often included command and signal centres, accommodation and logistic facilities.
Synaesthesia	Literally the ability for the senses to hear colour or see music and smell shapes. Also synaesthesia is the ability for one sense to trigger another, for example

music may trigger a memory associated with it which will trigger the taste buds to remember what was eaten when listening.

Tamping

Tamping is the term given to the fill placed behind a mine charge to avoid the blast funnelling back up the tunnel. Sandbags filled with spoil, or just spoil by itself along with large chunks of chalk, were usually used, piled to the ceiling and extending for several metres. A space was then left and the process repeated again, the number of times dependent on the size of the charge.

The missing

The intense destruction of industrial weaponry produced a new phenomena in warfare where soldiers could simply cease to exist. Artillery barrages could atomise men, leaving no visible trace of their bodies. Additionally, many were buried by shell fire and mine explosions, meaning that no remains for some of the dead have ever been found, and they have no known grave. These men are remembered on monuments across the landscapes of the war.

Wombat Mine

A hole drilled horizontally towards the enemy positions about 3-6 metres (9-18 feet) long and filled with explosives. When exploded, it created an instant deep trench across No Man's Land.

Zone Rouge

Before the conflict was over, plans were drawn up to cover the clearance of munitions, debris and matériel waste from the battlefields in anticipation of the reconstruction and rebuilding that would follow. The Western Front's battlefields were classified into three separate zones; Blue, Yellow and Red. Blue zones signified areas that could be returned to their pre-war use with relative ease; Yellow zones were places deemed to require a more thorough clearing, and Red zones were sectors where the cost, human risk and practicality of clearing the land outweighed the areas' intrinsic value. In the years since 1918, almost all of the Blue and Yellow zones have been cleared of war debris and are today accessible to the public. Even the Red zones (*Zone Rouge*) were repeatedly reassessed after the war, as pressure grew from landowners and the ability to clear these areas became more refined. Areas of the Meuse seen as suitable for returning to farmland were still being cleared for human occupation as recently as 1976 and even today unexploded munitions are regularly pulled from the land either by accident, or as part of a continuing effort to rid the old battlefields of their hidden dangers. Particularly dangerous parts of the Western Front are still regarded as belonging to the Zone Rouge.

Modern Conflict Archaeology

THE SERIES

Modern Conflict Archaeology is a new and interdisciplinary approach to the study of twentieth and twenty-first century conflicts. It focuses on the innumerable ways in which humans interact with, and are changed by the intense material realities of war. These can be traditional wars between nation states, civil wars, religious and ethnic conflicts, terrorism, and even proxy wars where hostilities have not been declared yet nevertheless exist. The material realities can be as small as a machine-gun, as intermediate as a war memorial or an aeroplane, or as large as a whole battle-zone landscape. As well as technologies, they can be more intimately personal – conflict-related photographs and diaries, films, uniforms, the war-maimed and 'the missing'. All are the consequences of conflict, as none would exist without it.

Modern Conflict Archaeology (MCA) is a handy title, but is really shorthand for a more powerful and hybrid agenda. It draws not only on modern scientific archaeology, but on the anthropology of material culture, landscape, and identity, as well as aspects of military and cultural history, geography, and museum, heritage, and tourism studies. All or some of these can inform different aspects of research, but none are overly privileged. The challenge posed by modern conflict demands a coherent, integrated, sensitized yet muscular response in order to capture as many different kinds of information and insight as possible by exploring the 'social lives' of war objects through the changing values and attitudes attached to them over time.

This series originates in this new engagement with modern conflict, and seeks to bring the extraordinary range of latest research to a passionate and informed general readership. The aim is to investigate and understand arguably the most powerful force to have shaped our world during the last century – modern industrialized conflict in its myriad shapes and guises, and in its enduring and volatile legacies.

THIS BOOK

The First World War was precisely that – a global conflict fought in all of the world's physical spaces, in the air, at sea, on land, and - as Matthew Leonard shows us in this meticulously researched book - in the dark, airless and lethal depths beneath the infamous battle-zones of the Western Front in France and Belgium.

The subterranean war which Leonard explores is as unsettling and alien as it is unknown to the majority of those with an interest in the First World War. Yet underground fighting was an integral part of the conflict, linked to the deathly struggles on the surface, albeit endured by far fewer men. All along the old Western Front today are the hidden remains of conflict below ground. Unlike the rolling countryside above, where time and society has softened the scars of war, or re-packaged the battlefields for heritage and tourism, the visceral places of 1914-18 survive just a few metres below. It is as if there were two wars, one tamed and altered and accessible to today's visitors and researchers, the other a jagged, uncomfortable, and sometimes lethal entity, lurking surreally in tunnels, caverns, and passages beneath – and for the most part inaccessible, and often unexplored. Many certainly still remain to be discovered. In recent years, several of these subterranean places have been opened to the public, providing a glimpse into the past, but mainly there is a vast underground universe where the clock has stopped and only a few have ever ventured within.

During the war, the surface and subterranean worlds shared primeval conditions created by the modern technology of high explosives. Death and injury could arrive unannounced, comrades manning trenches disappeared in an instant, atomised into nothingness. Yet underground, there was a unique challenge to human senses – men gasped in suffocating space, and developed new sensitivities of smell, sound, and touch in conditions where human vision was often of little avail. Deprived of sight, sound became a dominant feature of the subterranean war experience. Not the fury of artillery and aerial bombardment which dominated the surface fighting, but a deadly quiet, where hearing and recognising faint noises, characteristic sounds, and silence itself, could be the difference between life and death. Men had to re-learn the world, how to move, how to communicate, how to survive.

Yet there was also a deeper, metaphysical dimension lying behind the military formalities of battle plans, digging tunnels, laying charges, hanging gas curtains, and clay-kicking. Tunnellers of the First World War, and those that accompanied them underground were entering a dark realm of myth and spirits locked into human consciousness and beliefs from time immemorial. The First World War may have been the world's first industrialised global conflict – a harbinger of modern ways of killing – but it was no less 'ancient' and unnerving in some of its landscapes and places – especially those below the surface. Regardless of race, nation, ethnicity or religious belief, underground was most often regarded as a place for the dead, not the living. In one of the curious yet lethal realities of the First World War, where the world was literally, as well as metaphorically, turned upside down, soldiers were safer beneath the surface than on it. Hell, it seemed, had been moved by war from the subterranean depths to the world above; yet the doubts still remained – millennia of human beliefs about the denizens of the underworld could not so easily be shaken off.

And then there are the traces of humanity which the underground worlds of war have preserved, in sometimes astonishing detail and variety. Many of the places explored in this book have been sealed from everyday life for a hundred years – and have served as time capsules of a century-old war. Graffiti and carvings capture a moment in time, and an individual's response to it. Sometimes they are memorials, perhaps the last written comment or artistic flourish of a life about to be cut short. Documenting and analysing these marks today is anthropology and archaeology as much as it is history, and moves the study of these signs of war beyond mere recording, and into the realm of emotion and memory – freeze-framing a human life in time, and sometimes too connecting to real people through identifying the maker and perhaps tracing living relatives as well. There is an intensely human satisfaction in making such visceral connections between the living and the dead, and in a sense returning ancestors to the present even if only fleetingly.

Compared to a century of historical research, and innumerable books concerned with the military history of the First World War, the extent and nature of the underground war is largely unknown to the public. It is a feature of the author's own research underground as well as in libraries and archives that he can bring academic rigour, personal experience and an interdisciplinary approach to the subject.

Here is a voice of authority which comes from having shared the subterranean world with the ghosts of those who fought, suffered, and died there a hundred years ago. The author's contribution here is all the more incisive and boundary-pushing because it is embedded in the wealth of experience and insight provided by the Durand Group of underground war specialists, of which he is a member, and which has spent decades exploring and researching these places beneath the Western Front, quietly, professionally, and without fanfare. There is no glory-seeking amateurism here, nor chasing of television cameras – only a serious respect for people, places, knowledge and understanding. It is this combination of qualities which makes this book such a valuable and insightful guide not just to the harsh physical realities of the underground war, but to the new and unexpected dimensions which these men encountered, and to which they had to adapt, first to survive, and then to carry out their duties. The author's achievement is to guide us in through these new experiential places, on a voyage to the nether worlds of the Great War for Civilization, and to bring us back transformed.

Nicholas J Saunders,
University of Bristol, July 2016

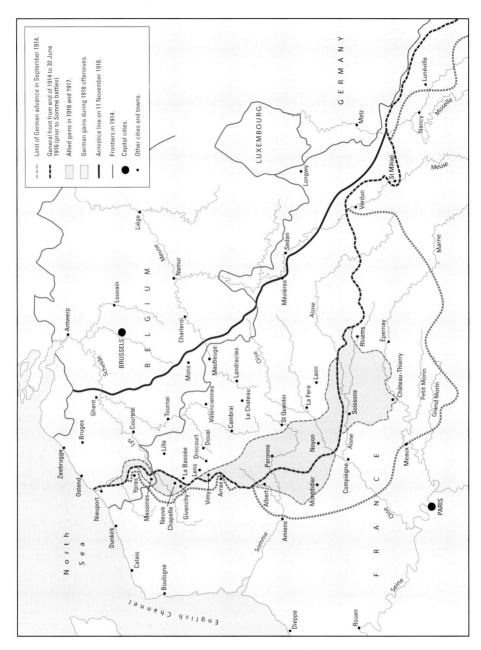

The Western Front 1914-1918

Introduction

This book tells the hidden story of subterranean warfare on the Western Front, discussing the existential realties of being underground in a modern war. How did this new environment affect the human psyche or the ability to prosecute the war? How did these worlds feel, smell, taste and sound? These questions are answered through the melding of disciplines, by engaging anthropological theories with archaeological fieldwork – through a modern interdisciplinary approach to the material culture of twentieth century conflict.

Much of the research for this book is taken from my own fieldwork, a great deal of which has been conducted with my Durand Group colleagues. The subterranean worlds of the Western Front offer a chance to experience some of the last remaining visceral and untouched landscapes of the conflict. They are rich in material culture, and without the ability to spend extended periods of time in these places it would not have been possible to approach the underground war in such a holistic manner.

A hundred years after its beginning the First World War is still a conflict that most find difficult to comprehend. The common idiom portrays the years between 1914 and 1918 as a slaughter, and often a callous one at that. The few strips of grainy film footage that show soldiers rushing out of their trenches are endlessly recycled, almost always accompanied by the sombre tones of television presenters describing the fate of these figures walking to their doom. That some of the most famous film clips are in fact not of soldiers going into battle at all, but of training exercises or re-enactments, matters little – after all, the vast cemeteries and grandiose monuments that now cover the old battlefields support the perceived realities of the pointless massacre of so many.

Perversely, the Second World War, although far more bloody than its predecessor, is not viewed through the same lens. Far more were killed and injured, atrocities committed by all sides were greater in number, civilians were targeted in huge volumes by relentless bombing campaigns, invasions, occupations, internment camps and ultimately, atomic weapons. There were as many terrible failures of military judgement in the Second war as in the First. Germany's Russian campaign (Barbarossa) and the Allied invasion of Holland (Operation Market Garden) were the result of flawed decision-making, just as were the fateful invasion of Gallipoli in 1915 or the conduct of the Somme battles that raged in Northern France during the summer of the following year.

The reason for this disparity is overwhelmingly one of perception. The proliferation of film footage and photography from the Second World War, much of it in colour, appears to show how well combined arms assaults worked together. *Blitzkrieg* conjures images of a war of movement, and the weapons and tactics used resonate with modern interpretations of armed conflict. Importantly, the memories of many who were there, and are still alive, reaffirm these truths. Additionally, the Second World War has been the subject of innumerable books, films and television dramas over the past fifty years, embedding preconceptions and histories into the common consciousness. Thus the Second war is more familiar to us, analogous to the twenty-first century conflicts witnessed on current-day 24-hour news cycles. The viewer believes that they can 'see' events and thereby 'picture' the conditions in which the Second war's battles took place.

Conversely, the First World War, and particularly the Western Front, cannot adequately be imagined, so different was it to anything that had occurred before 1914, or since 1918. Despite the conflict's many theatres, the majority of the British involvement took place on the Western Front, the experience of which was not ruled by sight alone.[1] It was largely a static place, dominated by a corporeal experience of the landscape, a place registered by the eyes but not truly seen. The paucity of available visual media means that historians are required to rely on written evidence of life at the front, a turbulent mix of poetry, exquisite prose and musings of the common man. The language used in this literature is couched in the relationship between soldiers and the landscapes of modern conflict, and men regularly liken themselves to animals sliding or creeping through the muddy wastes.[2] What visual media there is to accompany this comprehensive literature reveals little, often no more than the confines of a trench or a blurred image of a desolate No Man's Land. Accordingly, the pejorative impression of the Western Front is of a place destroyed by artillery, and criss-crossed with ubiquitous trenches divided only by the empty space in between – a dead place where men suffered and died.

Military history has described the battles, weapons, tactics and strategies in detail, producing an understanding of how the war was fought, but little of the way it was actually experienced. The approach of traditional battlefield archaeology to the study of the conflict has been to excavate mostly-known positions to reaffirm existing truths. The objects found are then systematically catalogued, identified and finally displayed in a museum. In the early years of the war archaeologists were embedded with German front line troops, who scoured the spoil from freshly dug trenches, searching for artefacts to send back to their country's museums or to display for the entertainment of their troops.[3] Little appears to have changed.

These war-archaeologists were able to conduct their research in much the same manner that archaeologists had always done. In 1914 and early 1915 the full industrial might of the belligerents had not yet been fully realised, and the places being investigated had not yet become true modern conflict landscapes.

A century later, the Western Front requires a different method of investigation to that of pre-industrialised battlefields. It is not a static entity, rather it is a deeply complex and dynamic landscape, and it is also one of the most heavily contested places on earth. Today the old battlefields of Northern France and Belgian Flanders are a site of pilgrimage and memory, a landscape of cemeteries and memorials that favours some events over others, and prioritises the memory of the victors. It is a place for battlefield tourism and the associated financial ventures that cater for those who visit. Recreated, or completely invented areas of 'battlefield' entice visitors, offering them a taste of 'trench life'. Parts of the Western Front in France and Belgium are not even French or Belgian, but have been given in perpetuity to those nations that helped to defeat Germany in 1918. Many areas that saw bitter fighting are today bustling villages or towns, usually replete with a museum and a café serving war-themed food and drink as well as often spurious souvenirs.

Hidden from sight among these different stories of the war are the unrecovered remains of thousands of soldiers, sometimes buried, waiting to be discovered by farmers or building contractors, but more often just the microscopic remains of people destroyed almost utterly by artillery, mines and other industrialised weapons. They are 'the missing', those with no known grave, an invisible army of the dead, and an unheard of concept before 1914. So destructive was the conflict's weaponry that even today it still claims lives, and a defining feature of modern conflict landscapes is their continuing, potentially lethal, nature. In 2015 two workmen in Ypres were killed after unearthing a shell and trying to remove its copper drive band, and farmers regularly plough up shells, ammunition and other detritus every year during what is colloquially known as the 'Iron Harvest'.

The Western Front can often seem a confused mess of contrived narratives; local, national and international politics, different religions, commercial endeavour, mass death and continuing danger. It is a landscape that cannot be understood unless it is approached from a modern archaeological-anthropological perspective, one that acknowledges the complexity of twentieth century warfare, and the ambiguous and often esoteric landscapes and objects it produces. The Western Front is not only a huge artefact, but a palimpsest, a place where many different 'layers' make up the whole. Each is laid down on top of the other and each has the potential for many sub-divisions, and for more to be added in the future. By appreciating this layering of landscape it is easier to acknowledge that the Western Front has a social life, its own biography in which the story of how it has changed and adapted is recorded.

Although many academic disciplines must be marshalled to achieve a holistic understanding of the First World War, individually they present an incomplete picture, restricted by the limitations of each subject's academic scope. Additionally, many disciplines pay almost no regard to the complex relationships between landscape, people and objects, and how these develop over time. Engaging with the last century's wars from any singular perspective can often produce fundamental misunderstandings of the human experience of modern conflict. Before 1914, warfare was understood by the sense of vision, but afterwards was experienced by the whole body. Throughout the twentieth century, whether in a trench, a Lancaster bomber, a U-boat or a Chieftain tank, modern warfare demanded a total corporeal relationship with the environment for survival. This book will demonstrate that a reliance on vision and what is 'seen' blinds us to the physical and metaphysical realities of the Western Front. The hybrid approach of modern conflict archaeology adopted here combines disciplines such as archaeology, anthropology, military history, cultural history and literary studies without favouring or prejudicing any. By doing so, it is able to develop a more holistic understanding of the life and daily experience of a soldier on the front lines of the First World War.

Between 1914 and 1918 many new technologies were brought to bear, yet these did not always benefit the men who were living life in the earth of the Western Front. Aerial photography was born and then came of age above the battlefields of France and Belgium, yet for every photograph taken of the trench lines only a fraction of the front's defences could be seen. The trenches, so clearly defined from the air, represented but the battlements of a fortified castle. Beneath was a catacomb of tunnels, caves, subterranean quarries, cellars, listening positions, hospitals, chapels, command centres, stores, corridors for troop movement, and vast underground mines packed with tons of high explosive. The depth of this subterranean landscape reached over 100m in places[4], and underground systems were regularly constructed using concrete, metal, rubber and wood.[5] Many had hot and cold running water for the hundreds of men that sheltered in their dim glow, relatively safe from the carnage and chaos above.

To survive in this world, a place more akin to the Dark Ages than twentieth century Europe, required a complete renegotiation of the way the human senses understood the environment. Long accepted beliefs, implicitly held yet in reality only subliminally recognised, stated that sight governed the lives of human beings, and touch that of animals. This had to be reassessed in the dark, smoke filled, gas swamped muddy hell of the frontlines; yet at the same time, men could not be allowed to become 'animals' – the soldiers were there to fight a war, not regress to a prehistoric existence. So they constructed a new hierarchy of the senses, one that allowed them to understand the seemingly medieval conditions of the front, and simultaneously construct this place in ways they could understand.

Tunnellers built or adapted a subterranean world beneath the trenches, infantry usually accompanied them in their work, and all soon realised the benefits of digging into the earth for protection. Chapter 1 of this book provides an overview of this underground world so intrinsic to the Western Front, outlining the nature of this type of warfare. The role that subterranean places played in every day life and several of the major battles is explained, as is the formation of the tunnelling companies, revealing the type of men involved. Importantly, underground warfare through the ages is also explored, showing how as conflicts became industrialised so the importance of this branch of warfare increased. From its tentative birth on the battlefields of antiquity to the extensive subterranean world carved out beneath the steaming jungles of Vietnam, men have fought in the darkness. Even today in the cavernous mountains of Afghanistan or beneath the Israeli border, the earth continues to be harnessed by those that would wage war. The industrialisation of conflict has made this practice more relevant, not less. Nevertheless, it is not the intention of this book to produce a definitive history of underground warfare, which is ably detailed in other publications.[6]

Chapter 2 explores the complex relationship that soldiers developed with the subterranean conflict landscapes of the Western Front. It discusses how the body and mind adapted to life underground, and how this is key to understanding the realities of daily life at the front. To the modern Western reader, primarily using any of the senses other than sight to understand the world is not easy to appreciate. Yet looking at other cultures, past and present, reveals that in many parts of the world this sort of interaction with the environment is commonplace, allowing parallels to be drawn, albeit cautiously, with the life lived below the front lines of the First World War. More than fifty-two different nationalities were present at Ypres in Belgium between 1914 and 1918, creating a potent mix of culture, religion and ritual practices. The varied ways in which war-life underground was perceived therefore differed considerably, and these ambiguities will also be investigated.

Chapter 3 tells the story of the Durand Group, a remarkable collection of individuals specialising in the investigation of First World War underground sites. Together, the Group has explored more than twelve kilometres (7.5 miles) of tunnels in recent years.[7] Archaeological research beneath the Western Front is a difficult, time-consuming, expensive and hazardous undertaking. Often engineering work is required above and below ground to make access safe and ensure there is a controlled working environment underground, both processes that require specialist skills. Modern conflict landscapes are always contested places, so before any excavations can begin many different people, from mayors to landowners, must be consulted and permissions sought. Just finding tunnel entrances often involves considerable prior research, and when underground, often in deep, and very constricted spaces, a team mentality is essential. As a result of these dynamic processes it is not possible to conduct this type of research alone.

Chapter 4 is the first of three case studies, each exploring a different section of the Western Front and examining how approaches to subterranean warfare influenced the course of battles, the war and the body and mind of those that fought. Chapter 4 investigates the Loos battlefield, demonstrating how far apart the British and German attitudes to subterranean warfare were in 1915, and how and why the Loos sector developed almost exclusively underground after the calamitous battle that taught the British hard lessons about the nature of industrialised war.

The second case study explored in Chapter 5 reviews the build up to the April 1917 attack on the German positions atop Vimy Ridge. In one of the most successful assaults of the entire war a combined British and Canadian force routed the Germans, and mastery of the underworld was intrinsic to this Allied success. Many of the lessons of Loos and the Somme battles of 1916 had been learned, and the mistakes of the previous two years would not be repeated. The scale of the subterranean engineering around Vimy was staggering, with numerous subways, fighting systems, listening tunnels and souterraines either constructed or expanded in preparation for the battle. This created a place where soldiers at the front could spend almost their entire time underground, relatively protected from the mechanised arsenals that laid waste to the surface. The experience of inhabiting this world, how it felt to wait in the subways before zero hour, or live in the souterraines of Neuville St Vaast is key to understanding how it was possible to conduct such an effective frontal attack, yet not take the casualties so associated with the war's other great battles.

Chapter 6 presents the third case study and steps away from the British experience of the underground war to look at the clash between Germany and France at Verdun. Many aspects of the battle have their roots in the subterranean landscape, whether in the huge forts that ringed the citadel, the deep underground bunkers used to shield the German storm troops before the attack, or the brutal mine warfare that occurred at Vauquois as part of the ten-month long fight for the 'heart and soul of France'.

Although many of the subterranean elements of Verdun are tangible, others are not. The intensity of the fighting, the size of the battlefield, the enmity between the protagonists and the overwhelming reliance on heavy artillery created a unique landscape at Verdun. It became a place where it was at times impossible to distinguish between man and landscape, the surface and the underworld, and even who was friend or foe. The war continued for almost two full years after the battle ended, yet never again reached the tortured intensity of Verdun.

The underground places explored in these case studies are the repository for many items of First World War material culture ranging from bullets and grenades to old newspapers, items of uniform and equipment. Each space is also home to many different examples of graffiti and intricate carvings, artefacts that say much about the morale, thoughts, attitudes and daily realities of those that occupied these subterranean conflict landscapes. Many of these artefacts have not been seen for almost a century, yet what they say about a soldier's life at war differs considerably from much of the written poetry and prose so inextricably linked to our ideas of the First World War. These objects have been rediscovered, yet they will never be placed in museums and the public will not be able to admire first hand the craft, artistry and emotion that went into their creation. They are part of the ambiguous conflict landscape of the Western Front, and like so much of the war's history, they are hidden from view.

Underground warfare was an integral part of trench warfare and the Western Front could not have existed without it. Life beneath the surface offered a respite from the terrible destruction above and a potential way around the stalemate and attrition of the trenches. The idea that life at the front was lived in the earth is not a new concept and has been recognised since the war itself. Much of the classic literature refers to it, although often it is implied or referred to obliquely – so much was it part of daily life that it was rarely expressly stated. In one of the finest books on the conflict, *The Great War and Modern Memory*, Paul Fussell describes the Troglodyte existence at the front, demonstrating how men in trenches and dugouts sheltered in the earth. This hellish existence changed the way that soldiers sensed their surroundings. Santanu Das, In *Touch and Intimacy in First World War Literature,* developed the idea that touch became an ever more important sense used to experience and feel the conflict. Conversely, Eric Leed, in *No Man's Land: Combat and Identity in World War One* examined how hearing replaced sight, allowing for the front to be mapped aurally. Das' touchscapes and Leed's soundscapes form the foundations of a corporeal examination of the war, and are central to an anthropological investigation of the soldier's daily life. Touch and hearing both increased in importance, and became essential to 'mapping' the earthen passageways and dugouts beneath the surface.

The crucial change was the way the senses now operated together rather than alone. In this book I build on the seminal research and insights of Das, Leed and Fussell through first-hand experience of these subterranean places to explore and show how during the First World War the majority of life was lived out of sight, and waged with all the human senses, in the darkness and claustrophobia of a world beneath the killing fields.

Chapter 1

An Overview of Underground Warfare

Before and after the First World War

The Western Front represented the culmination of subterranean warfare but it was by no means the first time it had occurred, and as early as 850 BC the Assyrians had developed a 'Corps of Engineers' specialising in underground attack.[1] In 334 BC Alexander the Great used mines at the siege of Halicarnassus and again to great effect two years later in Gaza.[2] During the first century AD the Roman writer Vitruvius described an advanced method for attacking fortress walls from below by digging tunnels, packing the space with wooden props and then setting them alight, collapsing the ground above and with it the enemy's walls.[3] It is thought that the defences of Jericho were felled by an Israelite mining operation that likely employed these tactics.[4] At Marqab, Syria, in 1285, the Knights of St John were so stunned by the extent of the Egyptian mining operations against them that they surrendered without giving battle. Once the tunnel had been driven below their fortifications and packed with explosives the Egyptians allowed the Knights' engineers to survey it and to see for themselves the 'drastic consequences that could follow the firing of the mine'.[5] In the nineteenth and early twentieth centuries subterranean warfare increasingly formed an important part of siege warfare and the practice was constantly improved upon and developed.

During the Russo-Turkish War in 1828 acts of underground warfare were a common occurrence and amongst the many mines detonated were two of 4000 kg (8818 lbs). Mines of this size drastically affected the landscape and for the first time lessons could be learned as to how these huge explosions altered the surface terrain for good or bad, or hindered the explosion of other mines due to the intense vibrations the detonations produced.[6] Important experience was also gained as to how mine warfare could be combined with infantry manoeuvres, knowledge that proved to be invaluable during the Siege of Sebastopol in 1854.[7] Here, the Russians used subterranean explosives to disrupt a Franco-British attack, blowing around twenty mines of up to 2000 kg (4409 lbs) in tunnels driven through a strata of clay just beneath the chalk subsoil.[8] Mining was also a feature of the American Civil War, most notably when on 30 July 1864, a 155 m (511 ft) tunnel was completed beneath the Confederate position known as

Elliot's Salient and a 3600 kg (793 6lbs) charge was detonated, killing more than 300 Confederate soldiers.[9]

The Franco-Prussian War of 1870-1871 was over too quickly for mine warfare to be of much use, but during the Russo-Japanese War of 1904-1905 things were very different and the use of underground explosives accelerated.[10] The most notable example was during the siege of Port Arthur on the Liaotung Peninsula in Southern Manchuria. Here the Russians had initially captured the town and its surrounding forts, only to be besieged themselves by the Japanese. Over the course of six months the Japanese bombarded the fort with their ineffective artillery and launched countless frontal attacks to regain the forts, all to no avail. The Japanese changed tack and from late 1904, they dug more than 100 m (0.3 miles) of tunnels towards and beneath the Russians for the purpose of laying mines under the fortress's walls. In a portent of what was to come during the First World War this sparked intense underground activity as the Russians similarly constructed defensive tunnels to fend off the attackers, creating a tense situation underground in which 'both sides listened carefully and did what they could to muffle the sound of their own picks and shovels'.[11] Nevertheless, the Russian efforts were ineffective and the forts, and then the town, finally fell on 2 January 1905. Many nations, including Britain, France, Austria and Germany followed the events in Manchuria, gaining experience that would be essential on the Western Front only a decade later.

Since 1918, mining operations and subterranean warfare have been deployed on numerous occasions. In the Philippines during the Second World War, General MacArthur set up his command post on Corregidor in the Malinta tunnel beneath the island's fortress.[12] Four thousand troops crowded there to escape the intense Japanese bombardment and the dust-laden heat and stench from hundreds of wounded stagnated the air.

During the battle for the Pacific, on many islands the Japanese defenders constructed a labyrinthine system of tunnels to defend against the American Marines. Nevertheless, these confrontations were generally more fluid than in the First World War, meaning subterranean defences could not hold out for long, and there was no time to attempt an undermining of the enemy's positions with explosives. Even so, while the underground defences did hold out, they were still an effective means of keeping the enemy at bay and protecting the defenders. On the Pacific Island of New Britain the huge defensive position known as 'Fortress Rabaul' was underpinned with hundreds of miles of defensive tunnels, allowing the Japanese to fight almost to the last man.[13] Similarly, on Peleliu the Japanese linked up caves and trenches with tunnels, allowing for speed of movement, rapid (and safe) access to stores and supplies, and the launching of night time attacks.

In the tunnels beneath Mount Suribachi on Iwo Jima, the Japanese kept a garrison of over 1,200 men and their commander, Kuribayashi, had his headquarters in the deepest part of the island's tunnel system.[14] Lieutenant

General Kuribayashi Tadamichi also ordered his men to create a substantial system of tunnels, linking up bunkers and caves that stretched for over 25 km (15 miles) beneath the island.[15] Similar situations occurred on Peleliu in 1944[16] and Okinawa in 1945.[17] The use of tunnels to link defensive positions was one copied from the First World War's Western Front, and the sensorial impact on the mind and body were similar. Yet the climate in the Pacific differed from that of France meaning that malnutrition, malaria, and dysentery sapped at the will to live and produced a nervous order of its own known as 'tunnelitis'.[18]

Later in the twentieth century during the Vietnam War (1955-1975) the Viet Cong guerrillas relied on tunnel systems to shelter them from the immense firepower brought to bear by American forces. The Vietnamese had an intimate relationship with their landscape that Americans found difficult to grasp and so successful were they that for a long time the Americans remained completely unaware of this underground battlefield beneath their feet. Famously, the Americans even built a major base at Cu Chi directly above an underground tunnel system that had existed since the days of the Viet Minh struggle against France in the 1940s and 1950s.[19] This underground war differed markedly from that of the Western Front. There, the opposing sides each sort protection below ground from mutually destructive weaponry, thereby experiencing a similar and simultaneous corporeal experience while learning to appreciate the nuances of life in a subterranean landscape. To the Vietnamese, however, the land had always been seen as 'a source of life… the basis for the social contract between the members of the family and hamlet or village'.[20]

This was a reality the westernised Americans struggled to understand. The Viet Cong created a modern conflict landscape, completely hidden from view, that the US military had no knowledge of. Many Viet Cong fighters rarely set foot on the surface unless attacking the enemy – Major Nguyen Quot spent the greater part of ten years living underground.[21] Cooking, sleeping, and surgical operations all took place in the tunnels, and children were even born there. This, potentially, life-long sensorial relationship with the landscape was completely alien to the Americans, used to life in the United States of the 1960s and 1970's

The Viet Cong saw themselves as human beings doing what was necessary to resist a powerful invader. This sensorial juggling act was the direct result of soldiers' understanding of their battle-zone. Yet in Vietnam the two sides lived very different lives. The Communist forces knew their country intimately, and to them the jungle was part of their culture, yet the Americans found it inhospitable, preferring to spend the majority of their time in huge firebases, only venturing out on patrols or to seek the enemy out in force. By doing so they cut themselves off from the environment they were fighting in. Once the Americans discovered the existence and extent of the Viet Cong's subterranean landscapes they were culturally and militarily ill prepared to counter the threat, and many Americans tasked with flushing out the guerrillas from their tunnels felt their humanity slipping away in the underground world. As they entered the cramped and dark passageways to seek out the enemy, the bestial senses took over, 'I was just an animal – we weren't human beings – human beings don't do the things we did, I was a killer rat with poisoned teeth'.[22] These US soldiers even referred to themselves as the 'Tunnel Rats'.

During the Cold War in Europe, many used the sewer systems that ran under the Berlin Wall to escape from East to West and when these were shut off, escapees dug numerous tunnels instead.[23] In the twenty-first century in Gaza, tunnels are regularly carved out beneath its borders with Egypt and Israel. The first of these were dug during the late 1960s as hiding places, but they quickly developed into a method of smuggling contraband. In September 2001, Palestinian guerrillas exploded a tunnel bomb under an Israeli checkpoint[24] setting in motion a system of attacks that harked back to the Western Front. As the border between Israel and Gaza is (more or less) static, tunnels can also be utilised as mortar positions, again akin to the way they were on the Western Front. The number of tunnels in use is uncertain, but between January 2013 and August 2014 the Israeli Defence Force uncovered 36 running under the border[25], demonstrating that even in modern warfare tunnelling is still significant.

Beneath the Mexico/US border tunnels are regularly used for smuggling purposes, often outwitting the vastly technologically superior American authorities. Osama Bin Laden's use of the Tora Bora caves in Afghanistan further demonstrated how the sensorial creation of landscape, and the understanding of its complex layering could be an effective weapon against an ignorant enemy. The main cave of the complex was allegedly outfitted 'with an armoury of Kalashnikovs, a theological library, an archive of press clippings, and a couple of mattresses draped across several crates of hand grenades'.[26] Taliban forces in Afghanistan have used hidden cellars to store weapons and ammunition and the extent of their use of subterranean features is yet to be fully realised.[27]

Although subterranean warfare existed before 1914 and has proliferated through many aspects of twentieth and twenty-first century conflict, the manner in which it has been waged has changed little. Tunnels have always been dug as quietly as possible, these features have been used for both attack and defence, and their construction and habitation has required a revision of the sensorial engagement with landscape. Before 1914 many of the lessons of underground warfare learned in the late nineteenth century and before were put into action, and the sheer extent of the Western Front's subterranean landscape provided a rich source of knowledge for the combatants of future conflicts.

The First World War on the Western Front

The Western Front during the First World War produced the greatest scale and sophistication of underground attack and defence the world has ever seen. This was the first truly modern conflict and it fundamentally changed the way that warfare was conducted. In large part this was the result of the industrialisation of warfare and the technological advances this enabled. Battles could now last for months, changing the notion of a battlefield into one of a battle-zone. The hitherto undreamt power of the weaponry deployed consumed landscape, humans and matériel in vast quantities, and to escape the destruction on the surface of the Western Front soldiers burrowed ever deeper into the ground creating an extensive subterranean element to conflict. The underground war was a logical progression of trench warfare on the Western Front. The proliferation of modern weapons such as the machine gun, chemical weapons, high explosive and large-calibre artillery meant that attacking enemy positions across open ground was fraught with dangers, as demonstrated by the hitherto unimaginable scale of the casualties suffered in France and Belgium by all sides.

Underground operations began on the Western Front as soon as the trench lines formed, although initially they were intended to be purely defensive. As early as October 1914, the French began constructing dugouts along sections of the Argonne front to protect the *poilu* from relentless artillery barrages. They also dug out into No Man's Land, installing countermines to deter the enemy should he be digging towards them.[28] Initial French attempts to undermine German positions south of the River Somme at Dompierre failed;[29] but not to be deterred they tried again in the Argonne, amidst repeated German attempts at countermining, and detonated perhaps the first of their mines on 13 November 1914.

The first underground attacks on the British Expeditionary Force sections of the Western Front occurred on 20 December 1914 at Festubert on the Somme, when the Germans exploded ten small mines beneath the Sirhind Brigade of the India Corps who were holding that section of the British line.[30] At the time the Indians had been trying to undermine the Germans further north, which ultimately failed, yet even so the British forces were ill-prepared to wage this kind of warfare, but the attack at Festubert spurred them into action. For those manning the trenches life was difficult enough without the fear of being attacked form below. Something had to be done.

While the German specialist Pioneer Battalions were inching their way closer to the Sirhind Brigade in France, across the Channel in Britain, one far-sighted Member of Parliament had already considered the benefits of waging war underground on the Western Front. Major John Norton-Griffiths (later Sir), as well as being an MP, was the head of a large engineering company that had a great deal of experience digging tunnels for utilities under major cities including London and Manchester. The method used to construct these tunnels was known as 'clay-kicking' and involved a man leaning back on a 'cross' and using a special spade to remove spoil from the tunnel face. Norton-Griffiths was convinced that this digging method was suited to the clay of Flanders as it was fast and quiet, and accordingly he wrote to the War Office on 15 December 1914 to inform them of his idea.[31] The timing was fortuitous, yet the response from G.H.Q (General Head Quarters) was less than enthusiastic - the general consensus being that civilian mining was a very different prospect to digging in the confines and dangers of the Western Front.

Grafting Tool   Clay Kicking or Working on the Cross   The Cross

Clay kicking was well suited to the clay of Belgian Flanders, although the clay kickers had to learn new techniques in the harder chalk and sandstone elsewhere along the front. (© **Public Domain**)

Despite the British reticence to pursue the subterranean war, the Germans pushed ahead with their underground operations, blowing numerous small mines opposite the Brickstacks on the Cuinchy section of the line near Loos in northern France.[32] The German tactic was to follow up the mining with swift attacks, capturing strong-points and trenches, and fortifying the crater lips, merging them into their lines. For the rest of the war the Germans remained supreme at this tactic, and try as they might the British and French never quite managed to emulate their skills.[33] It was clear even in these early stages of the Western Front's existence that the war would be taken underground, and that the British had a lot to learn. Norton-Griffiths worked tirelessly to promote the merits of subterranean warfare and despite early opposition, High Command soon saw the wisdom of his ideas.

Sir John Norton-Griffiths was the driving force behind the creation of the British and Commonwealth tunnelling companies, and would tour the front lines in his Rolls Royce inspecting the subterranean works. (© **Public Domain**)

German underground activities in early 1915 spurred the British into action, and in truth the British Command had little option. For soldiers manning the trenches, the dangers were ever-present. By early 1915 it was apparent what the immediate future held for the Western Front. Defence lines had started to settle down, positions became fixed and the use of artillery escalated. This made life increasingly uncomfortable for those in the front lines, but it was the fear of being attacked from below that started to alarm those facing the enemy. To get men to stand in appalling conditions and defend a trench against attacks was difficult enough. They were exposed to artillery fire, the elements and the sight of hundreds of men charging their positions. But the difficulties in attacking entrenched defences meant that often attackers would be decimated before they even reached the first line, bolstering the confidence of those manning the parapets. The real fear was of being blown up from below with no warning. It played on nerves, made men jumpy and diminished their fighting capability.

The exact layout of defensive positions varied depending on the terrain, but in general there were three lines of defence on both sides. The front line trenches faced each other across No Man's Land. Behind these were the support trenches, ideally 180–280 m (200-300 yards) to the rear. The third line, or reserve line, trenches were the same distance further back. The three lines were connected by communication trenches and saps, and listening positions and machine gun posts would creep out from the front line into No Man's Land. Forward trenches on the British side were designed to be approximately 2.5 m (8 ft) deep and 1.5 m (5 ft) wide with sandbags built up on the side facing the enemy (the parapet), ideally to a height of 1 m (3 ft) above the surface.[34] In front of the forward most positions lay a field of barbed wire, usually with bits of old metal, shrapnel or food tins attached to it to announce the presence of raiding parties approaching in the dark. The barbed wire was a formidable obstacle and backed up by ever-alert machine gunners, snipers and increasingly effective artillery, attacking these defences was almost impossible without considerable loss of life.

In early 1915, Allied and German trenches remained basic, despite both sides having regulations and manuals concerning their construction. The Germans had the advantage of topography however, as they had been able to choose the best ground, often overlooking French and British lines, and facilitating their construction of subterranean fortifications. Men would often sleep in the side of trench walls, in positions known as 'funk holes', little more than hollowed out pits just smaller than a man. Soon, dugouts were constructed, small rooms that slept a few officers and offered some protection from the metallic air. Before long these were enlarged and increased in number, allowing men of all ranks to seek refuge below ground, in albeit rudimentary accommodation.

Once the Schlieffen plan had failed, and their advance had been checked on the Marne, the Germans had no intention of giving up the terrain they had captured – if the British and the French wanted it back they would have to take

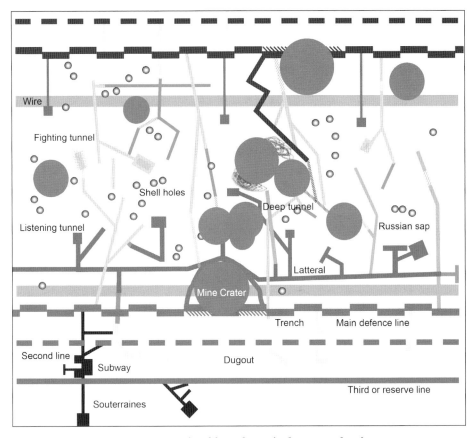

Much of the Western Front remained largely static for years, but it was not stagnant. No Man's Land and the trench systems that bordered it were in a constant state of flux as tunnels, trenches, dugouts and saps were constructed, destroyed and then recycled. (© **Author**)

it by force. This was exactly what the Allies intended, and as a consequence their positions were going to be far less permanent than the German equivalents. German trenches developed into substantial defensive positions. By 1916, on the Somme some of the German dugouts were over 10 m (30 ft) deep and could sleep dozens of men. They were built using concrete, steel and wood, often had running hot and cold water, cooking facilities, electric lighting, wallpaper, furniture, and even doorbells next to the steel doors that protected their entrances.[35] Many of the abandoned houses in the shattered local villages were ransacked for anything that would make life more bearable, and soon all manner of decorations from mirrors to beds were being dragged underground, humanising the traditional home of the beast. This created a new hybrid home of looted war debris and objects underground – a distinctive kind of conflict-related materiality and 'domestic' space. As the war progressed the Germans had more time to create these elaborate structures, with many of the units occupying the same positions for years.

The British and French underground spaces were far less luxurious by comparison. The Command could see little point in constructing comfortable lodgings for men that were supposed to be evicting the Germans from France and Belgium, and indeed too much comfort would hardly be conducive to getting the troops to attack at all. British trenches were often rudimentary, drained through a combination of basic wooden constructions involving an 'A-frame' covered with duckboards. Dugouts were shallower and more hurriedly prepared, and they rarely contained the luxuries of German positions. The French trenches were even worse, with little attention paid to even the most basic sanitary provisions. As Sassoon remarked about the Allied positions, 'when all is said and done, the war was mainly a matter of holes and ditches'.[36]

As the conflict progressed through 1915 and beyond, the ability to not only live below ground but also defend from subterranean attack gained importance. Norton-Griffith's plans had been put into action during the second year of the war and were already starting to pay dividends. By June 1915 the 8th British tunnelling company (178 Tunnelling Company) had been deployed, and a year later mining operations were being conducted along almost two-thirds of the British front.[37] There were now thirty-three tunnelling companies in the British complement; twenty-five Imperial or British, three Canadian, three Australian, one New Zealand, and the Australian Electrical and Mechanical Mining and Boring Company (known as the Alphabetical Company – for obvious reasons!).[38] The French and the Germans were conducting a similar volume of underground construction and it is estimated that at the peak of activities, in the summer of 1916, that there were likely some 120,000 men on all sides directly involved in constructing life and landscape beneath the Western Front.[39]

The numbers involved and the need to escape the increasingly lethal conditions on the surface meant that the subterranean front lines became ever more sophisticated. Undermining the enemy became seen as a way out of the intransigence of trench warfare and developed into an integral element of many major engagements including the battles of the Somme in 1916, the encirclement of Verdun (1916), Arras (1917, of which the attack on Vimy Ridge was a major component), the Aisne (1915 and 1917), and Messines (1917) where mine warfare reached its most devastating level. Smaller mines were detonated on an almost daily basis along the Western Front to hinder the progress of enemy miners or to gain a tactical advantage in No Man's Land and all this announced an increasing complexity and dynamism of the subterranean conflict landscape.

To the British, underground warfare was seen first and foremost as a defensive undertaking. The Germans had stolen a march during the early months of the conflict and the fear of being attacked from below was very real to the British infantry. The tunnelling companies' first job was to shore up the British lines.

Wherever possible they did this by constructing a tunnel parallel to, and just in front of, the British lines. These tunnels were known as laterals, and although depths varied, they were driven deep enough to mean that the Germans would have difficulties digging beneath the lateral, thereby diminishing their potential to undermine the British trenches – something that was made even harder by the positioning of listening posts at regular intervals. The lateral not only ensured that the trenches received some protection, it also acted as a jumping off point for offensive operations. Fighting tunnels, designed to silently creep beneath No Man's Land made their way from the lateral to the German lines, as did dummy tunnels designed to fool the enemy sappers, and further 'fighting' tunnels constructed to seek out the enemy's tunnels.

Offensive mining developed for a multitude of purposes. Small 'camouflet' charges were used to bring down the enemy's offensive tunnels without breaking the surface or affecting friendly tunnels. Larger mines, eventually consisting of up to sixty tons of explosive[40], were used to devastate enemy positions and many mines were detonated in No Man's Land to create a tactical advantage. In these cases the purpose was to advance positions into No Man's Land or to create or cut off a salient. As soon as the mine was detonated the attackers would rush out of the trenches to capture the far lip of the crater, allowing them a position from which they could dominate the enemy. Although this was a regular occurrence, the British were continually amazed at how fast the Germans could react to their attacks, and then commence a counter-attack of their own.

The idea of huge mines being detonated in No Man's Land, leaving vivid scars in the landscape, paints a pronounced, if not misleading, picture of the subterranean war. One of the most visited places on the Western Front today is the Lochnagar mine crater at La Boiselle, the physical echo of an enormous charge detonated as part of the British attacks on the morning of 1 July 1916, a day forever associated with death and destruction. Eight minutes before the Lochnagar mine went up, Geoffrey Mallins, the British officer charged with filming the grand attacks, famously captured the detonation of the Hawthorn Ridge mine a few miles to the north. The crater it formed is still visible today, yet it lies beneath a large copse of tress and is heavily overgrown with vegetation, making it far less noticeable than Lochnagar. Both these mines were but two of the twenty-three detonated that morning (although six were much smaller in comparison to the other seventeen), but the physical craters made by the others have largely since been reclaimed, either by the nature or local farmers. The modern day visitor to the Somme is easily led by this presence of absence, which in turn confuses the tactical and strategic necessity of mines. Indeed despite the proliferation of mining taking place by mid-1916, the co-ordination of detonations with infantry attacks still left a great deal to be desired. Mine detonations often caused problems for the attacking infantry, either by disturbing the ground to be attacked across, or by giving the Germans an advantage when they (inevitably)

The Lochnagar crater at La Boiselle on the Somme is as impressive as it is misleading. The subterranean world of the Western Front was as much about attack as it was defence. (© **Author**)

captured the crater lips first. It would be another year before the British perfected the integration of mining with infantry assaults and artillery barrages.

In the northern sector of the British attacks the trench lines were in places around a quarter of a mile apart but shallow tunnels, known as Russian Saps, had been dug beneath No Man's Land, designed to allow small groups of men to appear seemingly from nowhere in front of the German trenches. Ironically, the secrecy involved in digging these tunnels meant that the infantry did not know of their presence. As the first waves of attacks went in tunnelling company officers who had crept out and created exits from the shallow tunnels were horrified to turn and face the British lines and see the ranks being cut down before they even reached the sap-heads. It showed just how disjointed the idea of combined operations was. Mines were being blown with increasingly regularity, yet the purpose of these detonations was often confused, and this confusion was by no means confined to the Somme battlefield. At Vauquois near Verdun, between 1915 and 1918 more than five hundred mines of varying sizes were blown on a hill that measured no more than 460 m wide by 340 m deep (1509 x 1115 ft). Here mine warfare had taken on a life of its own and between the French and the Germans more than 17 km (10.5 miles) of tunnels, to a depth of over 100 m (328 ft) in places had created a literal version of Hell. Mining was carried out with such regularity and ferocity that in the end a truce was called, with neither side prepared to continue. The story was similar from Flanders to the Alps, yet these offensive mines were only a minor part of the subterranean story. As the thunderous sounds of the large mines exploding resounded across the Somme, the majority of the German defenders along the line were still sheltering from the artillery barrages deep below the surface in their dugouts, analogous to the manner in which the American forces utilised the Malinta tunnel in the Philippines during the Second World War. The Germans were about to prove to the British the real benefits of a close corporeal engagement with the subterranean battlefield.

On the morning of the 1 July 1916, the 87th Brigade of the 29th Division attacked Y-Ravine across what is now the site of the Newfoundland Memorial Park at Beaumont Hamel. The positions had been bombarded for days, but as the British advanced, the shaken and largely unharmed soldiers of the German 119 (Res) Infantry Regiment were able to clamber up from their deep dugouts, establish their machine guns, call in artillery support and stop dead (literally) the four advancing battalions in No Mans Land. A follow up by the 1st Battalion of the Newfoundland Regiment and 1st Battalion of the Essex fared little better.

The 1st Battalion of the Newfoundland Regiment suffered over 90% casualties in just 30 minutes on the morning of 1 July 1916. The area of No Man's Land they attempted to cross has been preserved largely in tact. (© **Author**)

The main defensive position at Beaumont Hamel. For more than two years the Germans had been constructing deep underground bunkers in the Ravine that were impervious to the British bombardment that proceeded the Battle of the Somme. **(© Author)**

All along the Somme front the situation was repeated, proving that despite the spectacular sight of thousands of tons of earth mushrooming up from the ground and obliterating the German trenches, it was really the defensive art of underground warfare that decided the day.

For the most part, the Germans had focussed on strengthening their positions along the Somme front, knowing that a major attack there was inevitable. By the summer of 1916, their underground systems were far more comprehensive than those of the British or the French, whose resources were largely committed to offensive action. Many of the same German units had occupied Y-Ravine since 1914, and for two years they had been carving out a system of tunnels and deep dugouts in the chalk, allowing them to survive the British bombardment when it finally came. The defensive philosophy displayed by the Germans at Y-Ravine was not the exception, it was the rule, and, as this book will show, it was a lesson that the British would quickly heed.

After the Somme battles of 1916 British tunnelling operations were incorporated more closely and effectively into offensive planning, but more importantly the deeper earth was increasingly used to protect soldiers from the dangers of life in the trenches or on the surface further behind the lines. Many of those that perished on the 1 July 1916 never saw the enemy. As soon as the initial attacks went in the Germans began to remorselessly shell the rear of the British positions, choking off reinforcements as they were brought up. Most of these were advancing across open ground, seemingly too far from the front line to be in danger, but the longer range artillery still caused devastation amongst their ranks. The mistake was not repeated and the relative safety the German defenders experienced in their deep shelters did not go un-noticed either. Existing caves, cellars and underground quarries right across the front were seized and expanded by the engineers, not just British, but French and German, too. They were linked to more forward positions by trenches or tunnels, allowing men to travel underground for long distances, relatively safe from harm.

When the Battle of Arras opened on 9 April 1917, less than a year after the infamous first day of the Somme, up to 24,000 Allied troops lay in wait below the town of Arras, ready to be funnelled into the front line trenches. The situation was repeated on Vimy Ridge, where on the same day a predominantly Canadian force with British support attacked along more than a dozen subways[41] that had been constructed by the British tunnelling companies. In the Loos sector, after the catastrophic British attack of September 1915, virtually all activity had retreated underground. At Messines, in 1917, the detonation of nineteen huge mines was

The Wellington Mines beneath Arras were expanded by the New Zealand Tunnelling Company. By 1917 the British had learned to protect men underground before they went into battle. (© **Author**)

The Spanbroekmolen mine crater on the Messines Ridge. The mine was one of nineteen exploded along the Ridge during the initial 30 seconds of the 1917 Battle of Messines. It was detonated slightly out of sequence, so debris the 'size of houses' fell on the attacking troops as they charged the shattered German lines. (© **Author**)

intricately co-ordinated with artillery support and the infantry assault, ensuring one of the most spectacular successes of the war. The lessons of 1916 had been learned.

Increasingly, life began to be lived underground, and battles were waged from beneath the surface too, changing the relationship between the soldier and the battlefield. This new experience of warfare required a renegotiation of the way soldiers thought about, navigated and understood their world. Far from the experience being one of muddy trenches, it was one of chalk walled or wood planked spaces deep below the surface, where sight faded from importance, touch became a way of life, and hearing, smell and taste took on new meanings.

A modern archaeological-anthropological approach to the investigation of the subterranean battlefield is taking our understanding of daily life on the Western Front in new directions, allowing for a more nuanced and insightful appreciation far removed from the one-dimensional perspective of the 'trench'. Military history has informed us of the way the war was fought, and battlefield archaeology has excavated the remains of the materiel used, but it is modern conflict archaeology that shows how the tactics were implemented and experienced, what the relationship was between man and materiel, and most importantly, how it was that so many men could live in such an alien environment and not only survive but form a coherent and effective fighting force.

Different nations constructed their underground worlds according to their own distinctive cultural parameters. Size, depth, and the materials used in construction all show the different approaches to a life underground. German systems tended to be well engineered and extensive, and well suited to the requirements of defensive warfare. The French systems were shallow and often, although not exclusively, poorly constructed with little thought spared for those that lived there. British systems were more effective, and designed to first and foremost defend from attack in order to facilitate aggressive moves towards the enemy. This cultural connection to landscape can be seen not only in the physical statistics of tunnel systems, but also in the innumerable items of graffiti and carvings found on their walls, material culture that still contains the traces of those who created it.

German graffiti tends to be informative, well sign-posted for the most part, along with neatly written names and dates. French graffiti, as graphically demonstrated in the Confrécourt Quarries near Soisson, often feature religious iconography and symbols of national or military pride, and these are regularly found interlinked with one another. British markings are often simply names and dates of the 'Tommy was ere' variety. American carvings and graffiti demonstrate

Graffiti and intricate carvings are commonplace beneath the Western Front and are deeply cultural artefacts. A French soldier in the Maison Rouge souterraine beneath the Chemin des Dames battlefield created this image, likely during 1917. (© **Author**)

how keen the troops were to get involved in the conflict, and show the faith they had in their country's ability to 'win the war'. Perhaps most interesting of all is the Canadian graffiti, which tends to contain a myriad of personal information. Name, rank, regiment, service number, home addresses and other personal information are regularly left, and the style of many carvings reveals much about the pride Canadians took in being at war, a fledgling country carving out a role for itself in the new world.[42]

Occasionally, as in the Froidmont souterraine on the Chemin des Dames, several nations occupied the same space at different times, providing a direct comparison between the different nations' graffiti. Here, the French, German and American forces all left graffiti on the walls at different times, and interestingly none of the writing or intricate carvings have been vandalised, perhaps a reflection that despite cultural differences, all realised that the deprivations of modern warfare were felt by everyone, regardless of nationality. First World War graffiti can be seen as being generically similar to modern urban graffiti, which was originally regarded as vandalising urban spaces but is now valued culturally and commercially as mainstream art. The work of urban artists such as Banksy can be compared to that of First World War soldiers such as Private Ambler (see Chapter 5).

Along the Chemin des Dames ridge (so named as Louis XV built a path across the ridge for his daughters to use) there are over 370 known souterraines, and although by no means all have been entered (or even located) since 1918, it is probable that most were appropriated by the forces that clung so desperately to the slopes of Louis XV's 'Ladies Way'. It was in 1917 that on this elevated section of terrain stretching between the Aisne and Ailette valleys the French would suffer as the British had done at the beginning of July the previous year. During the Somme battles the French had adopted different tactics to the British, relying on the superiority of their artillery and in particular their adept use of the 75 mm field gun. Almost a year later it was as if the French were going backwards, failing to appreciate the lessons of the previous three years fighting. On 9 April 1917, amidst the swirling snow showers that blanketed the battlefield from Arras to Soissons, General Nivelle, hero of Verdun the previous year, launched his grand offensive, the one that was to win the war, declaring 'We have the formula… victory is certain'.

As the British attacked at Arras and a combined Canadian and British force

In the Froidmont souterraine on the Chemin des Dames French and German graffiti can be found side-by-side. Graffiti and carvings were rarely vandalised by the enemy, perhaps indicating how men on all sides empathised with the other's situation. (© **Author)**

smashed into the German defences on Vimy Ridge, the French huddled in their trenches and stared at the imposing ridgeline in front of them – there was not a German to be seen. The German lines were being mercilessly pounded right along the entire 80 km (50 mile) front, as 1,200,000 men, 5,000 guns, 200 tanks, 47 squadrons of artillery-spotting aircraft, 39 observation balloons and 8 squadrons of fighter planes all swung into action. Much of this force was deployed along the Chemin des Dames front, but it had little actual effect. The Germans had captured Nivelle's battle plan two weeks previously, and the French general's tendency to boast at dinner parties meant that much of his strategy was in open circulation.

Even so, the overwhelming firepower at Nivelle's disposal could still have made the difference if the French had better appreciated the value of subterranean warfare. It was here that their laissez-faire attitude to the war underground would prove fatal. As when faced with the British on the Somme the previous year, the Germans had taken full advantage of the local geology, and adapted existing souterraines, dug deep stollen (concrete lined underground bunkers) and ordered their front lines to be evacuated. The 5 million shells poured into the now-empty German positions did little more than break up the ground over which the French infantry was to advance, and the Germans, sheltering deep below the surface, remained physically, if not mentally, untouched by the huge bombardment. This shattered terrain rendered the rolling barrage designed to precede the infantry almost useless, and not because the attacking poilu could not keep up with it, but because it fell woefully short and the ground was so bad that the men could not outrun the bombardment.

Once the heaviest shelling had abated, the Germans climbed up to the surface from their protective shelters and machine-gunned the French from the front and rear. So effective were the German underground defences, and so destroyed was the ground that the French passed over many of the tunnel and dugout entrances without even knowing they were there. Their focus was not on what was going on beneath their feet, but on their own artillery barrage raining down on them from above. It is estimated that the Germans had 100 machine guns for every kilometre of the battlefield; and they ripped the French infantry to pieces. At the end of that first day, the French had suffered over 40,000 casualties.

'The attack gained at most points, then slowed down, unable to follow the barrage which, progressing at the rate of a hundred yards in three minutes, was in many cases soon out of sight. As soon as the infantry and the barrage became disassociated, German machine guns… opened fire, in many cases from both the front and flanks, and sometimes from the rear as well'.[43]

It was almost a mirror image of what had happened at Beaumont Hamel in July 1916 and despite what had now become a forlorn hope, the attacks continued over the coming days, during which, in a Herculean effort, the 69th Battalion of the French colonial Senegalese Infantry managed to reach Hurtebise Farm on the top of the Chemin des Dames ridge, where it was annihilated, almost to a man. Enough was enough and on 21 May 1917, the 21st Division mutinied, many others followed and the French could have lost the war.

The German superiority in underground warfare played a pivotal role in the Second Battle of the Aisne, and the mutinies that followed. The fact that the massed might of the French Army had done so little damage to the Germans was completely demoralising, and it was clear that the French had learned little from the British or their own experience at Verdun, where the German use of deep stollen had been so effective. The French suffered some 187,000 casualties on the Chemin des Dames before the offensive was called off, and by that point in the war they should have known better.

After the battle, the mutinies were quelled and General Philippe Pétain, the new commander of the French armies in the northeast (and also a hero of Verdun) began to restore order. Nevertheless, the Chemin des Dames became the scene of one of the most insidious instances of the war below ground. The battle may have been lost, but the French could not afford to weaken their force, and the Germans would eventually have to be weeded out of their underground lairs. They began to probe the ridgeline for weak spots, and at a place where it narrowed, not far from Hurtebise Farm, they encountered a large German force sheltered below ground, protected by cannon and machine guns that poked up through the corpse-ridden ground, spewing fire on any who approached.

The Germans had first entered this former underground quarry in 1915 and immediately set about strengthening it and constructing further entrances and exits – seven in all. Once the required weaponry had been installed at each of these locations the Germans christened the souterraine the *Drachenhöhle* (Dragon Cavern), after the fire that poured forth from each entrance. Below ground, the Germans created sleeping quarters, dug a well, and installed a first aid station. A chapel and a cemetery were also constructed and electric lighting illuminated the gloomy cavern. On 25 June 1917 the French finally managed to gain a foothold in one of the entrances and slowly, at exorbitant cost, began to push the Germans deeper into the souterraine. Eventually, the French got far enough in that the two sides had to share the same underground space. Each set up internal walls to protect from the other, and the war continued underground, 15 m (45 ft) beneath the surface. Surprise attacks were launched, gas was used, the electricity failed and terrible hand-to-hand fighting took place in the darkness.

Instances of one side breaking into the other's tunnel system were fairly commonplace across much of the Western Front, but these incursions were brief, isolated and quickly repelled. The situation at the Dragon Cavern was unique, and this subterranean landscape produced an equally unique sensorial engagement between man and nature. The conditions replicated the war above, but in the claustrophobic darkness below. All the senses were working at their

During late 1917 both the French and the Germans occupied the Drachenhöhle, constructing internal walls, laying barbed wire and flooding the souterraine with gas. The war continued below ground as it did above. (© **Author**)

limit; the nose constantly searching for the telltale whiff of gas, or the distinct odour of the enemy. The darkness strained the eyes, making it harder to tell if the man approaching was friend or foe, which in turn made the sense of touch ever more critical. Every sound could signal an attack, but these noises were not heard through listening equipment, pressed against a constricted tunnel wall, but with the naked ear straining into the black void. The nerves of those on both sides were strained to breaking point as the body and mind struggled to adapt to an environment far beyond that which human beings had ever imagined. It was the subterranean war at its extreme – a mixture of corporeal overload and sensorial deprivation, in a modern conflict landscape that had no parallel.

The situation at the *Drachenhöhle* may have been unique, but subterranean warfare was intrinsic to the existence of the Western Front, and it came to define the front line experience as much as artillery barrages, lice or the all-consuming mud. Without an appreciation of the scale of this hidden landscape it is not possible to adequately approach how the body and mind engaged with the landscape, or the extent to which the senses were able to negotiate the physical and mental demands of the Western front. So alien to modern Europeans was the First World War soldier's existence, that it must be more fully explored before the relevance of this 'war within a war' can be understood and given its rightful place in the history of the conflict.

Chapter 2
Assaulting the Senses

Imagine living in the earth surrounded by death, violence and almost unimaginable destruction. This is what life was like on the Western Front, a strip of utterly devastated land 10-25 km (6–15 miles) wide, stretching some 500 km (310 miles) from the English Channel to the Swiss border.[1] Outside this zone of death, life was often untouched by the war, but to soldiers with little or no view of the world outside their trenches, the shattered landscape they inhabited could seem a world without end. Charles Edmund Carrington, a young British officer who experienced the 1916 Battle of the Somme, wrote after the war, 'In fifty years I have never been able to rid myself of this obsession with No Man's Land and the unknown world beyond it. On this side of our wire everything is familiar and every man is a friend, over there, beyond the wire, is the unknown, the uncanny'.[2] Parts of the front in Belgium were less than 160 km (100 miles) from London, yet these areas had more in common with medieval interpretations of Hell than twentieth century Europe. The extreme violence of the conflict 'ruined the idea of ruins'[3] as it mercilessly destroyed everything in its path. Whole towns ceased to exist, vaporised by artillery, wiped off the map.

Henri Barbusse, in his seminal war novel *Under Fire (Le Feu),* describes how the once peaceful villages became characters in themselves, mirroring the fate of those who sheltered amongst their ruins. Poterloo, one of Barbusse's main protagonists, is a soldier who before the war had lived his whole life in the village of Souchez. He finds himself fighting nearby, while the French made super-human efforts to capture the strategic heights of the Lorrette Spur and Vimy Ridge. During a lull in the fighting he ventures back to his home village to find the house he has lived his entire life in, yet what he finds is nothing like he remembers:

> The village has disappeared, nor have I seen a village go so completely. Ablain-Saint-Nazaire and Carency, these still retained some shape of a place, with their collapsed and truncated houses, their yards heaped high with plaster and tiles. Here, within the framework of slaughtered trees that surrounds us, as a spectral background in the fog, there is no longer any shape. There is not even an end of wall, fence, or porch that remains standing; and it amazes one to discover that there are paving stones under the tangle of beams, stones, and scrap-iron. This – here – was a street. It's

there – no, I've passed it. It's not there. I don't know where it is – or where it was. Ah, misery, misery![4]

Barbusse paints man and the shattered landscape of the front as being one image, entwining the two together. Souchez and Poterloo are indistinguishable from each other, the fate of each framed through the oblivion of endless mud, utter destruction, and the hopelessness of war. So intense was this destruction that soldiers soon came to empathise with nature as it suffered from this death of landscape.[5] The war did not distinguish between men, objects or the land, all were destroyed without mercy. Yet from this destruction came creation, as new relationships were crafted between men and their material culture, and new landscapes were born from the remnants of the old. The once verdant fields turned into endless quagmires of mud, shattered equipment and the rotting bodies of men and horses. The living and dead shared the same space, and notions of life and death were literally inverted – the dead lay strewn across the surface of the front, while the living survived deep in the earth, interred through a necessity to survive.

When soldiers arrived on the Western Front they encountered a place where their prior rules of sensory engagement no longer applied. This was an environment that could not be understood in the same way as a modern European city or town. Aristotle's notions as to the order of the human sensorium, the group of human senses, which had been accepted for thousands of years, were questioned by the realities of the Western Front. Here, a reliance on sight could prove lethal, and an intimate relationship with touch or understanding of sound could be a lifesaver.

Just existing in this lethal place demanded a complete renegotiation between body, mind and landscape – and it was one that had to occur quickly. Our senses allow us to understand the world we live in – more than this; they shape it and guide us through. Today, our understanding of the world is primarily visual. Signs point the way to destinations, shops illuminate their doorways with recognisable logos or write their names in attention-grabbing designs. Lighting and signage guide us. Life is lived through the eyes.

Nevertheless, our other senses play a vital role in understanding our world. Sounds alert us to danger. Noxious smells likewise serve as an early warning system, while pleasant odours may attract us into coffee shops or supermarkets – and even to each other. Touch, the animal sense according to Aristotle's long accepted law of the senses, allows us to feel safe or unsure, soft furnishing makes us comfortable, streets are smooth making driving or walking easier. Soft is safe, hard is not, blunt objects inspire touch while sharp or serrated items make us feel aware. Life is lived and understood by the way the senses interact with and create the world around us.

Perhaps more important to understanding this relationship between people and their world is the realisation that the way the senses engage the world is cultural. We understand this relationship because the senses transmit 'cultural values' to us from an early age. The way people and societies sense is the way they understand.[6]

Sight

The other senses compensate when sight is denied. In complete darkness, humans quickly apply touch to adjust to the new environment. In effect a visual sense is 'born in the fingertips.... The knees see. The elbows see. All admire the variations in velocity that differentiate light from sound'.[7] With no light, touch often takes over as the main human sense and people adopt a more feral sensorium to navigate the world. This change in the sense order caused by the absence of light has been observed by neuroscientists conducting experiments on how blindfolded able-sighted volunteers begin to show physiological changes in the brain after as little as five days. The other senses quickly compensate for the lack of sight, with initial enhancements in tactile-spatial sensitivity and awareness often occurring within ninety minutes.[8]

The laws of physics offer a critical perspective on sight because the objects and landscapes we see with our eyes are not actually seen at all – it is only the reflection of light from objects and landscape that gives them visual form and definition.[9] In the absence of light, or in poor lighting conditions, human sight becomes virtually useless. Above ground, in the sunlight, objects reflect light with ease disguising the way that subtle textures and knowledge of the environment are experienced by societies where vision is not dominant.[10] Descartes described sight as being the 'most noblest of the senses'[11], but he also declared that it is 'the soul that sees, not the eye' as vision is only actualized in the brain.[12] He explained how a blind man sees the world with the aid of his stick. When the tip of the stick touches an object, feeling is passed along it, through the nerves of the hand and is then processed in the brain. If two sticks (one in each hand) touched the object simultaneously, then knowing the distance between the hands would allow the brain to 'visualise' the object as though it were two rays of light reflecting its form. Touch is able to process 'visual' information in the same manner as sight, as the senses work in unison, not isolation, demonstrating the holistic nature of the senses. Life in the underground landscapes of the Western Front was a deeply sensorial undertaking, far removed in intensity and engagement from contemporary European life above ground, and modern life in the twenty-first century. Reliance on sight was a luxury that few could afford. Generals and staff officers may have been able to view the Western Front in safety through the new medium of aerial photography, but most never experienced the visceral conditions of the front line. Conversely, those in the front lines could see almost

Relying on vision offered little help to those in the trenches. It was quickly apparent that new ways of engaging with the environment would be needed. (© **Author**)

nothing, yet they felt everything.[13] Looking over the top of a trench was often suicidal. Sight lines along the trench were obstructed by their zig-zag design (known as crenalation), which was vital to stop trenches being enfiladed, or completely put out of action by a direct hit. This restriction of vision saved lives.

During the day soldiers lived below ground, protected from the dangers above, but at night the front came alive as work and raiding parties went into No Man's Land on work details, to bring back the wounded or silently slither through the mud and wire to attack the enemy's trenches. The ability to work in the dark was vital, so an appreciation of the power of sound, both its creation and detection, was essential. Even when soldiers left the trenches en masse to attack, very little could be seen through the chaos, smoke, explosions, gas and the masks worn to defeat it. Underground, either in tunnel systems or souterraines, light was always artificial and sometimes absent. No matter where men found themselves, sight was a sense that quickly became superfluous.

Light is therefore socially and culturally experienced, inhabited and manipulated. Even in a landscape devoid of natural light, some form of artificial luminosity is required for the eyes to function, and different forms of man-made light can change the meaning and understanding of an environment. It is difficult for us to imagine the relationship previous generations had with the illuminating qualities of the naked flame. Its colour is different to that of electrical light; the light of a candle bounces and flickers; it creates heat and has a soft aura. These differences in the qualities of types of light are an important aspect of archaeological research. Carvings, graffiti and even the underground spaces themselves appear different depending on the light they are viewed in. The First World War soldier would have experienced a subterranean space via candle light or dim electric lighting, where as a modern researcher would likely use powerful LED lighting, producing different impressions of the same space. Additionally, candlelight gives the feeling of a warmer environment when compared to the harsher and whiter light of LEDs. This allows spaces to be 'felt' through light. Nevertheless, whether natural or artificial, to the able-sighted without light there is no life, without the power of touch in the darkness there is nothing.

Touch

So useless was vision that even when No Man's Land could be glimpsed it often appeared so alien that the eyes were not capable of deciphering it:

> Mile after mile the earth stretched out black, foul, putrescent. Like a sea of excrement… It was one vast scrap-heap. And, scattered over or sunk in the refuse and mud, were the rotting bodies of men, of horses and mules. Of such material was the barren waste that stretched as far as the eye could see.[14]

In this environment, touch, much like sound, often became far more useful than sight. In the glutinous mud, weapons could be felt for quicker than they could be seen. The distinct form of a hand grenade or the difference between sharp flint and softer chalk could make all the difference to injury, life or death. The front could be 'felt' in other ways too, as Wilfred Owen described in a letter to

A view of No Man's Land near Courcelette, France during 1916. Rarely was there much to see in No Man's Land. All life sheltered underground, while on the surface there was only death and destruction. (© **Public Domain**)

his mother, 'I have not seen any dead. I have done worse. In the dank air, I have perceived it, and in the darkness felt'.[15]

In many European cultures the sense of touch is said to have played little part in defining human existence. In Medieval and Renaissance times, smell, taste and touch were usually associated more with animals than humans.[16] As soldiers dug themselves into the earth, and became increasingly animal-like in this regard, perforce they adopted 'animal senses' to navigate these new experiential worlds, and so became more bestial in their appearance, behaviour and attitudes, 'In what way have we sinned, that we should be treated worse than animals? Hunted from place to place. Cold, filthy and in rags… in the end we are destroyed like vermin'.[17]

Many non-European societies understand their world according to touch in a manner that Europeans find difficult to understand. The Tzotzil Maya of the Chiapas highlands of Mexico understand their world through the way that temperature is measured through touch, and organize their society accordingly.[18] Men are believed to contain more heat than women, and are therefore said to be superior, although at birth, both sexes are said to be cold, so babies are bathed in warm water, wrapped in blankets and even covered in hot chillies to give them life. Marriage, baptism and becoming a shaman are all acts that increase heat, and therefore power. Even illness is measured and treated in terms of heat. The Tzotzil are by no means unique in the way they order their material world. Temperature also plays an important role for the Azawagh Arabs, who associate their spirits with heat, and in parts of Morocco spirits are associated with cold.[19]

Touch comes alive when the places we encounter are unrecognisable and the space in which it exists is not ordered as we would expect.[20] This often stimulates fear, which itself can be allayed by the medium of touch. Members of a group who share an extreme event are calmed when touched physically or spiritually by the others involved.[21] The feet, as well as the hands, are able to explore and understand hitherto unknown landscapes, and temperature, type of terrain, moisture levels and vibration can even be felt with the feet, producing a kinaesthetic (the sensation of movement in muscles, tendons and joints) experience vital to mobility and life, a potentially life-saving element during the physical extremes of combat.[22]

People talk of feeling objects, of being touched by each other, and also of less tangible feelings, such as spirituality or kindness. This ability to experience the effects of touch emotionally as well as physically were explored in the classic Greek story of *Pygmalion and Galatea*.[23] The artist Pygmalion's lack of reciprocal touch he feels with Galatea only amplifies the fact that she is not real. Only when Aphrodite brings the sculpture to life is his love for his creation finally communicated through the medium of touch. At the front class barriers and Victorian ideas of touch were steadily eroded through the need to survive. Santanu Das' work on gender and intimacy during the First World War discusses

Stretcher bearers of the 9th Field Ambulance, asleep on the railway embankment in front of Thames House, near Zonnebeke Railway Station. The conditions at the front forced men to live in close proximity, huddling together for warmth or protection. (© **Public Domain**)

how soldiers at the front would often 'kiss' as a sign of reassurance, either to a dying comrade or for courage before going into battle.[24] It was common, too, for men to huddle and sleep close together for warmth and security in the exposed landscapes of the Western Front, allowing them to feel safer and more alive. These concepts of touch were magnified underground as emotions became heightened. As Das says, 'In the trenches of World War 1, the norms of tactile contact between men changed profoundly'[25], and this was even more intense below ground as men were packed together in close proximity, under the severest physical and psychological pressures. Whether on the surface or below ground, men were forced to spend long periods without seeing the opposite sex, and instances of homosexual activity occurred, although during the war only twenty-two officers and 270 other ranks were court-martialled for indecency.[26] The close sensorial proximity to others may well have influenced attitudes towards members of the same sex.

Touch is not just a means of interpreting space. It is also a way of defining cultural norms and rituals, and interacting with people. It allows us to experience what cannot be seen, to be touched by what cannot be physically felt, and to orientate the body in unfamiliar spaces. It is experienced with the whole body, making it not only the most dynamic of the senses, but arguably the most important. This is why touch plays such a central role in understanding how soldiers lives were re-shaped by the industrial intensities of the Great War, where new understandings of touch and physical contact were created by cramped physical conditions, large numbers of men in a limited space, nocturnal military operations, and most damaging of all, the loss of limbs which conducted the nerve impulses to the brain and translated physical touch into visual imagery.

Sound

The concept of conducting life without relying on the eyes maybe alien to us, but many disparate cultures, both present and past, share a very different 'view' of the world. Right up to the outbreak of the war, sound had played an important role in defining rural French communities for hundreds of years. Life away from the cities and towns was often dominated by the tone, volume and regularity of the local village bell.[27] It dictated the rhythm of daily life and defined community and culture. Bells would ring to announce the beginning and end of the working day, births, deaths, marriages and social gatherings. Local communities would pride themselves on the size and number of their bells, the sounds they made and how loud they could chime. Sound defined this world and even the very presence of the bells were said to keep demons at bay, reflecting attitudes to religion and changing beliefs in Europe in the period leading up to the First World War. Once the conflict began these bells largely fell silent, and as it progressed ever more of them were appropriated for their metal, turning objects of peace into the *matériel* of modern conflict. The familiar and comforting sounds of chimes were replaced by the noise of metal shell barrages; the world and its contents were being recycled.

At the front the lines were often so close together that the enemy could be clearly heard, locating a soldier in the wider landscape. Learning to re-evaluate

An aerial photograph taken in 1917 of the German lines near Messiness under bombardment. These artillery attacks traumatised the body and mind – the noise was overwhelming and the ground shook with each explosion. (© **Public Domain**)

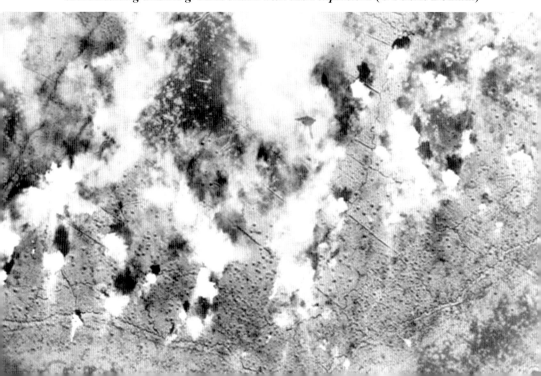

sound was a vital skill as attacks were often presaged by a change in the soundscape. The Western Front was a cacophony of noise. Rifle and machine gun fire mixed with the louder sounds of the artillery, and the sheer number of people meant there were also the shouts of the living and the screams of the wounded and dying. While this overwhelming noise remained, men were relatively safe, as major attacks usually occurred when the artillery stopped firing. This was the reverse of contemporary civilian life, where silence indicated relative safety and extreme noise, danger. Each kind of projectile had a unique sound, and hearing became so attuned that it was commonplace for soldiers to able to tell the type, range and probable landing place of each artillery shell as it approached, something that sight could not do. As one soldier put it:

> An expert knowledge of all the strange sounds of warfare, ignorance of which may mean death... My hearing was attuned to every kind of explosion... My nostrils were quick to detect a whiff of gas or to diagnose the menace of a corpse disinterred at an interval of months.[28]

Life in the trenches was intensely loud, and the restriction of vision meant that hearing became fine-tuned. However, an intensely loud soundscape means individual noises are difficult to isolate, which can cause disorientation, confusion and mental paralysis, something that was eventually realised to be the basis of shell shock.[29] Conversely, in a space with no sound, such as the deep tunnel systems of the Western Front and beyond, soldiers become disorientated akin to the way the deaf can often feel isolated, withdrawn, anxious and alone. For all human beings, the way the brain processes sound varies on the number of sounds being simultaneously absorbed. In a busy scene, the eyes record light being reflected and the brain processes this information with ease. Colours, shapes, and numbers are all calculated at the same time, giving an almost immediate understanding of the environment. Unless culturally adapted to do so, the brain doesn't process sound in the same way. Nevertheless, when it is quiet, and little or no light is present, the ears detect the slightest noise, identifying direction, location and source with relative ease, something vital for human survival in spaces deprived of light.

Language is primarily transmitted via sound, so hearing also has the ability to define our surroundings and relate it to us. The Western Apache share a unique relationship with language, naming places for how they were perceived, or events that had happened there.[30] Likewise, on the Western Front, trenches and tunnels were given names that reflected their location, danger and proximity to other objects. Sound is a medium that conveys language, place, danger, safety and culture. Beneath the Western Front, particularly in the claustrophobic fighting tunnels below No Man's Land, it was far more valuable than sight.

Taste and Smell

Even taste and smell are relevant to understanding the soldier's relationship with the environment, and again, an insight into the way that other cultures utilise these senses broadens our understanding of how the front lines were understood. The Ongee of South East Asia believe that smell is the fundamental cosmic principle[31], and illness is the result of too much, or too little odour. These olfactory beliefs govern life, death, hunting, ritual and religion. The Aztecs, lived in a universe governed by the life giving properties of water, which was given by the gods, and paid for with human sacrifice and frequent bloodletting. This was a multi sensorial existence in which touch, smell and mystique played a pivotal role.[32]

In parts of modern-day Asia life in many cities is still experienced through these mediums, reflecting the spiritual and cultural traditions of particular areas. In Japan, the smells from regional types of cooking form an olfactory map of many cities.[33] Similarly, the smells, tastes and culture of Filipino food create a home from home for the diasporic Filipino society of Hong Kong.[34] Through the sensorial experience of home cooking, a sense of place and identity is created.

Soldiers' food was always contaminated with mud, chalk, petrol, or even more unsavoury flavours. Often food, water, rum or wine had to be brought up to those at the front, and those tasked with carrying it ran extraordinary risks under fire. Sustenance would regularly not arrive, or would be partially or wholly lost on route as the porters dodged enemy fire or were killed, leaving the hungry and

Men of the 10th Battalion enjoying a hot meal near Eaucourt l'Abbaye, on the Somme during 1917. The front lines were a curious mix of smells and tastes, most of which were unpleasant. Note the petrol tins used to carry soups, stews, water and tea – receptacles that further contaminated the taste of food and drink. (© **Public Domain**)

tired men to imagine the smells of cooking or the taste of food that would never arrive.

There was a cultural element to taste and smell, too. Different nationalities would alter food according to their cuisine, and many attempts were made to improve the bland rations, creating powerful and distinctive odours across No Man's Land. HP sauce and Tabasco Sauce were favourites with many, used easily to spice up dishes, and these bottles are regularly found during archaeological excavations. Each nationality had a distinct odour. This was the result of the different detergents used to wash uniforms, soaps used by the soldiers, the types of tobacco smoked, food eaten and even the types of fuel used for generators, pumps and to start fires to keep warm. These different odours were cultural, but they were usually benign. The same could not be said for the poisonous gases used by all sides, an assault on the senses never experienced before in warfare. The two main types of gas used, phosgene and mustard, both had a very distinctive smell and were green or yellow in colour, so the senses were able to warn of the imminent danger. However, once detected, protective masks were donned that severely impeded some senses while simultaneously creating new sensorial experiences. The French soldier André Pézard wrote of the experience of wearing a mask during a gas attack:

> You do not see clearly with the glasses, which make you sweat around the eyelids. You have the mechanism, which dances on your nipples. The air heats up in the box of potassium. That scorches you from the bottom of your lungs to your kidneys. The brain begins to turn. The rubber cannula makes you want to throw up, and the saliva runs out of the corner of your mouth.[35]

This new danger was most prevalent in the trenches, but as poison gas was heavier than air it would regularly sink into shell holes or down steps into dugouts or tunnel galleries. As a result, every incline down into a subterranean system was fitted with two sets of gas curtains (one at the top and one at the bottom).

The senses then are essential to understanding life, and they allow the body to adapt to almost any situation, but the way that this interaction takes place depends on the environment people find themselves in. In the trenches, shell holes and mine craters that made up the lines, there was a stunning change in the sensory world. Smell and taste may not have been as important as vision or touch on the sensorial scale, but they were still senses that could save lives.

Sensing the deep

Below the trenches, in the deeper subterranean spaces, sensing the landscape proved to be equally challenging. Underground sound echoes easily and quiet

Three members of the British signal service wearing gas masks in a shell hole during a gas attack. Gas masks produced new sensorial experiences for soldiers, and many found wearing them unbearable. (© **Public Domain**)

noises seem louder, producing a radically different experience to life on the surface. Observing strict silence in many of these places was usually unnecessary as dugouts were located in trenches, the position of which was already known to the enemy, and large souterraines and caves were usually further back from No Man's Land, their approaches protected by laterals or other underground defensive workings. Likewise, subways were usually lit with dim electric lighting because candles would have been extinguished by passing traffic. Chambers were dug into the sides to serve as HQ's, medical posts and sleeping quarters, yet subways were claustrophobic, cramped and little could be seen apart from the man in front and the white of the chalk, or brown of the wooden walls.

In the deeper tunnels the ability to minimise noise was vitally important. Sound from the surface became muffled underground and at times non-existent – silence giving a feeling of safety – the opposite of life in the trenches. The noise made by men working underground could be felt through the tunnel floor and walls, as pickaxes and bayonets removed chalk, and equipment banged against tunnel walls. Even the sound of human voices and laboured breathing could be heard by those trained to listen for the approaching enemy. Listening tunnels were constructed at regular intervals and technologies were utilised to detect the approaching enemy. Geophones were employed to enhance the power of hearing, and in some places central listening stations were even linked to an array of seismomicrophones.[36] So powerful was this listening equipment that entire landscapes could be visualised from deep within the earth:

30 or 40 metres down, you can hear a stake being hammered into the floor of a trench as clearly as if you were beside the man driving it... Your ears gradually learn to interpret the sounds that reach them through the earth, recognising their origin, direction and distance away. That noise is coming from our trenches, but what about those dull thuds? Someone above us tapping a shoring frame into place. To the right, someone is working cautiously with a pick, and to the left another is stabbing into the face with a bayonet – there, he has just dislodged some clods of earth. Further away there is a humming sound – their electric ventilators are working. Then a buzzing sound: aha, they are using a drilling tool. Thus the sounds come to life for those who know how to read them.[37]

Fighting tunnels were necessarily small, often no more than 1.5m (5ft) high, in order to minimise the time they took to construct and the noise this construction produced. The size of these subterranean features required the human body and mind to adjust to the often-painful physical conditions on a daily basis. Compounding this problem was that the extent of the tunnelling operations meant it was common for one side to break into the other's system. When the opposing sides came face-to face these difficulties became amplified and hand to hand combat occurred in tunnels that were not even big enough to stand up in. In the dark, the only method of telling who was who was often to, 'feel if the man had any epaulettes; the Germans used to have epaulettes on the shoulder and we could tell that way'.[38]

Smells and tastes changed too. Chalk is a porous medium, which emits a fine dust, resulting in food and drink having a chalky taste, something very apparent after only a few minutes. In the wet, wood-clad tunnels of Flanders chalk dust was replaced with mud and these sensations were ever present in souterraines and dugouts, too, only increasing as the structures vibrated from artillery barrages, communicating taste via touch. The close proximity of so many people (some wounded, some dying) and the odours of sweat, urine and faeces mixed with those of field medications, food, hot drinks and tobacco, often created overpowering and ambiguous smells. Yet although the senses of taste and smell were heightened, they were not essential to survival – the degrading of vision and the heightening of hearing and touch still dictated the way in which the environment was primarily engaged.

The reordering of the senses meant that life-saving objects were often positioned so that they could be instantly located, minimising the time spent feeling for them in the dark. Weaponry was left at particular tunnel junctions, gas doors were regularly positioned in well-known places and instructions were carved in locations where artificial light was available, or at the beginning of new sections of tunnel to ensure that verbal passing of instructions was kept to a minimum and that these instructions would not be forgotten if sensory deprivation or lack of oxygen became a factor.

As the tunnel systems became ever deeper the amount of available oxygen was reduced. When oxygen levels fall below 18% human reaction times slow down, the senses become dulled, hallucinations can occur and the ability to function becomes severely limited. These environments could be so oppressive that no re-evaluation of the senses could hope to cope for extended periods. Animals also had to be used to accommodate for the weakness in the human senses, and canaries or mice were regularly taken underground by miners to alert them to the presence of carbon monoxide gas, a silent killer that the human senses are incapable of detecting.[39] The responsibility for maintaining human life was in effect transferred to non-humans, thereby reconfiguring their worth in the soldiers' eyes. Canaries and mice, animals previously considered as vermin or pets, were now the 'tunnellers' friends'.

Many of the advances in weaponry and technology that were utilised during the war contributed to reconfiguring mens' sensorium. The power of explosives, the multitude of different types of shell and the sheer number of rifles and machine guns assaulted the ears. Poisonous gas blinded, burned the skin and asphyxiated. The use of battlefield gas masks, hastily invented to protect against this new weapon, caused sensorial deprivation while at the same time were so uncomfortable to wear that they presented new sensorial challenges. Technological advances utilised for defence, such as the aforementioned seismomicrophones and geophones also affected how the sensorial scale was constructed and utilised. The adaptation of the human senses was being dictated by modern technologies, which in turn were causing the primitive and bestial conditions of the front, and allowing men to understand and relate to the subterranean world they inhabited.

Almost by definition, all life in the front lines was subterranean to a greater or lesser degree. This troglodyte existence, at least on the scale of the Western Front, was a novel enterprise, but many of those who created and inhabited these landscapes had previous civilian experience as either sewer builders or miners.[40] By 1914, more than 250,000 people were employed in the coal and mineral mines of northern England alone[41] and there were over a million miners across the United Kingdom as a whole. Clearly, daily life in the civilian mines of Britain differed considerably from the subterranean conflict landscapes of France and Belgium, yet it is valid to ask whether these men would have had some sort of corporeal advantage once they reached the front.

For the Victorian-era coal miner life was harsh and working conditions were often described as horrendous. Mines were difficult places to work, but factory workers, labourers and famers were also employed in cramped, unpleasant, dangerous and strenuous environments, which although were not underground, gave rise to similar sensorial experiences in the mines:

> Every organ of sense is injured in an equal degree by artificial elevation of temperature, buy the dust-laden atmosphere, by the deafening noise, not to

This German stick grenade **(known to the British as a potato masher)** *was found in the German T-19 tunnel system beneath Vimy Ridge. It had been wedged in a wall where the Germans feared a British break in. In the dark, life saving items were left in places they could be easily reached for.* *(© Author/Durand Group)*

mention danger to life and limb among the thickly crowded machinery, which, with the regularity of the seasons issues its list of the killed and wounded in the industrial battle.[42]

An Australian officer using a set of Geophones to listen for enemy diggers. The slightest sound underground could result in discovery and then being buried alive. **(© Public Domain)**

In the mines, people would regularly work in spaces as small as 2 m (6 ft) in height[43], and tunnelling was an important part of the creation of coalmines. To reach the coal seam many test tunnels were dug, and often engineering was required to protect from weak points and fractures. These difficult conditions forced the body to contort into unnatural positions, allowing many workers, and particularly miners, to experience kinaesthetic sensations which were later to be common in the trenches.[44] Despite the coal miners' familiarity with cramped spaces and adverse working conditions, their experience was of limited value in adjusting to life beneath the trenches. Although not required to undertake many infantryman's tasks, or adhere to military discipline to the same extent[45], miners were still given military uniform, rations, privileges and home leave as they were absorbed into the army, born anew as soldiers. They then had to negotiate the subterranean conflict landscapes in the same way as the soldiers who accompanied them underground. Any feelings of being comfortable in the earth would quickly be eroded as the realities of survival in this brutal landscape were brought into visceral focus by the war.

The way that miners were able to master the sensorial change between their civilian mines and the depths of the Western Front is highlighted in the lack of reported cases of nystagmus at the front. This chronic disease can occur when individuals are subjected to sustained periods in dimly lit environments. The eyeballs uncontrollably oscillate, causing sickness and headaches, and in Britain during the late nineteenth and early twentieth century it was a common occurrence in civilian mines.[46]

Despite the similarities between civilian mines and the subterranean conflict landscapes of the front, there were also differences. For the miners underneath the front lines the material they dug through and the tools they employed were not necessarily what they were used to, something that affected the feel of the working environment. The spaces they operated in were dynamic, varying from small fighting tunnels to vast expanded cave systems, all of which presented unique sensorial challenges. As the miners reached the more dangerous subterranean landscapes, a new appreciation of sound went in tandem with their revised understanding of touch– a notion as alien to the miners as to the infantry that accompanied them.

Experience of being in the earth gave miners an initial mental and physical advantage over common soldiers – many would have been working underground from a young age. Yet, because at the front all life was lived underground, and learning to do so quickly was a matter of survival, this advantage was short-lived. Once in the conflict labyrinth the realities and sensorial experiences of daily life differed so significantly from the miner's peacetime environment that previous experience held no advantage.

Tunnelling reports and war diaries offer a wealth of information on the physical nature of these systems and souterraines. Engineers meticulously surveyed these spaces, noting such features as angle of incline, internal tunnel measurements, the type and volume of construction materials required, and how many litres of water had to be pumped to drain deeper systems. All this demonstrates the importance and complexities of the underground war, yet while this technical information is welcome, these reports reveal almost nothing of the actual experience of being there.

The case studies that follow blend the military necessity and physical extent of subterranean landscapes with an idea of what life was like for those that had to live, work and fight underground. Much of the corporeal engagement described is the result of personal experience beneath the Western Front, more often than not with my Durand Group colleagues. The following chapter explores how the collective experience and knowledge of the Durand Group is revealing the secret landscapes of the underground war a century after they were abandoned.

Chapter 3

The Durand Group

The Durand Group is one of the most internationally respected organisations working on the Western Front today. A leading authority on subterranean conflict during the First World War, the group consists of professionals from the military (providing firearms and bomb disposal expertise) – some of whom have been decorated for their service, academics, archaeologists, First World War historians, mechanics, engineers, Health and Safety professionals, a documentary film maker, two medical doctors and three surveyors. The Durand Group is arguably the world's most experienced organization for the investigation of subterranean conflict sites. Academia's notorious unwillingness to 'cross disciplines' has at times been a hindrance, so perhaps it is no surprise that one of the organisations at the forefront of a new and holistic approach to the study of subterranean Great War landscapes is not academic at all.

Until recently, a dilemma has confronted historical and archaeological research into the First World War. To the historian, there is a plethora of material available ranging from trench maps to aerial photographs, personal diaries to official war records, battle plans to technical drawings, and a multitude of oral testimonies. In one sense, these items of material culture appear to tell the whole story, mapping out exactly what happened where, when and to whom. Alongside the written evidence, there appears to be a myriad of other objects to back up these sources. Artefacts from the conflict are numerous and many examples can be seen in the great First World War museums of Ypres (Ieper) in Belgium and Péronne on the Somme in France. Yet the conflict was one of matériel, a highly industrialised clash of armies in which the paraphernalia of war was produced on a vast scale. According to the Imperial War Museum, by the end of 1918 Britain alone had produced almost 4,000,000 rifles, 250,000 machine guns, 52,000 planes, 25,000 pieces of artillery and over 170,000,000 artillery shells.

Until about twenty years ago, the excavation of such conflict sites had been the preserve of traditional battlefield archaeology, which focused on investigating trenches or mass graves, which mainly served to reinforce the existing knowledge of military historians. The Great War was the first conflict to be documented by visual media. Photography from the air and in the trenches became commonplace. Aerial photographs in particular were used to produce precise trench maps, technical drawings and diagrams of defences and landscape, describing the military facets of the conflict in explicit detail. Film came of age, too, and moving images of life at the front further exposed the machinations of modern warfare to the public and military planners alike. Supporting this analytical evidence were thousands of personal diaries and memoirs, so it is valid to ask what the exposure of another trench in Flanders or Northern France can offer in the way of new information. It may well back up historical findings, but what else can it really offer the historical and archaeological record of the war?

This is not to say that military history and battlefield archaeology have no place in the modern interpretation of the First World War, far from it, and each has provided us with invaluable knowledge. But increasingly, these practices are being surpassed by more dynamic approaches to the study of twentieth century warfare that examine a wider range of topics, from the influence of aerial photography[1] to the relevance of food[2], the poppy[3], the role of women[4], trench art[5], the rehabilitation of the wounded[6], the power of sensorial interaction with landscape[7], and the cultural differences between and within the belligerent armies[8], to mention but a few.

As these varied approaches have developed it has become increasingly clear that the First World War is too complex, dynamic and multifaceted for one discipline to adequately narrate its histories. Modern conflict archaeology inherently recognises the complexities and ambiguities of modern warfare, and appreciates the potential of many disciplines' contribution to a holistic understanding of the conflict and its legacies, while at the same time prejudices none.

The Durand Group began in the late 1980s, when a team of Royal Engineers explored several kilometres of tunnel systems beneath the Canadian memorial

The Durand mine beneath Vimy Ridge consisted of 6,000lbs of ammonal in bags. The bags made the explosive easier to transport and store. In 1998 the mine's detonators were removed by Lieutenant Colonel Mike Watkins MBE. The process took more than 4 hours, during which Lieutenant Colonel Watkins was alone in the mine chamber, many metres below the surface. (© **Durand Group**)

site at Vimy Ridge. These explorations established that the war landscape underground was extensive and largely untouched since 1918. German and British systems were discovered, the latter containing two primed and detonated mine charges in almost perfect condition. One of these was the 6,000lb Durand mine located beneath a public area of the memorial site, a place visited by thousands every year. As if this didn't pose a big enough risk, archival research indicated the possibility of a much larger charge of 20,000lbs (the Broadmarsh mine) hiding deep beneath what is today a busy road junction.

These mines still posed a potentially serious risk. One of the defining characteristics of a modern conflict landscape is its enduring lethality, the potential to maim and kill many years after a war has ended. Before 1914, most battles lasted a day or less, and the battlefield was then cleared of the dead and wounded, and salvaged of munitions and weaponry. This was possible in part due to the way armies gave battle and then retreated or advanced from the field, but also because the ammunition used was inert after it had been fired. The technological advancements of the twentieth century created a new generation of armaments, far superior to that which it replaced. This new weaponry was then produced on a hitherto unimaginable scale. Many millions of artillery shells were manufactured by all sides, often to questionable standards, meaning a sizeable percentage (perhaps as much as a third) did not explode and remained live. During the seven days of bombardment preceding the 1 July 1916 (the opening day of the Battle of the Somme) the British fired some 1,500,000 shells in to the German lines to be attacked.[9] During the preliminary barrage for the Third Battle of Ypres (Passchendaele) the following year the British amassed 2,299 guns, one for every five yards of front to be attacked – ten times the density of the Somme barrage.[10]

Bullets were produced by the trillion, likewise grenades, and all manner of explosives, mine charges, booby traps and other methods of killing. Such was the volume of this expenditure that even a century later parts of the former battlefields are still littered with buried, unexploded munitions, many of which contribute to the annual 'iron harvest' collected by farmers every year. In some parts of the old Western Front there are so many unexploded shells that these areas have remained sealed off because they are too dangerous to clear. The French government estimates that there may be up to twelve million unexploded shells lying just below the surface in the forests around Verdun alone, and each year across the Western Front people are maimed or killed by these lethal reminders of the power of modernity.[11]

In June 1955, one of the unused mines laid for the Battle of Messines in 1917 exploded during a thunderstorm and it was fortunate that there were no human casualties (allegedly only a cow was killed). Although thankfully not a common experience, this was by no means an isolated incident. Late in 2015, without any apparent cause, a substantial amount of explosive detonated under a field around

10 km from Arras, leaving a large crater. The potential for these huge charges to cause harm is clear.

In 1996, Andy Prada, Managing Director of Fougasse Films Ltd and an independent filmmaker, met with Lieutenant Colonel Philip Robinson, who had conducted the initial investigations beneath the Vimy site with the Royal Engineers. Prada was keen to make a documentary on the Battle of Messines, with a particular focus on the mine charges that were unused that day and still remain dormant.[12] After their initial discussions it was clear that the remaining Messines mines posed too great a challenge so it was agreed that the documentary should focus on the Vimy mines instead. Fortuitously, at the same time, Veteran Affairs Canada, who had become increasingly concerned about the volume of explosives lying beneath their memorial site at Vimy, asked Robinson and Prada to ascertain the volatility of the charges during the course of making their documentary. A small team of specialists accessed the system and discovered that although a substantial quantity of explosives remained (in the form of boxed and tinned ammonal) the firing mechanism system had been removed from the mine, meaning there was no chance of a detonation occurring. The mine charges still lie beneath the ridge to this day, although they now are rendered harmless and most visitors to the site are unaware of their presence.

The success of these initial investigations beneath the Vimy battlefield prompted one team member, Lieutenant Colonel Mike Watkins, MBE (a leading

Lieutenant Colonel Mike Watkins MBE is remembered on a small but fitting memorial at Vimy Ridge near the entrance to the Grange Tunnel. His vision and legacy is continued today through the Durand Group. **(© Andy Prada)**

international expert in explosives and a member of the Royal Logistic Corp) to propose the formation of a specialist group that would continue research into the First World War's subterranean landscapes. Shortly afterwards, Watkins successfully removed the decaying detonators and primers from the Durand mine, rendering that inert, too. As a consequence, the fledgling team adopted the name 'Durand Group' and this unique organisation promptly began to reveal many of the hitherto little-known subterranean aspects of the Great War.

These experts continued to support Veteran Affairs Canada and investigated many kilometres of tunnels beneath Vimy Ridge, but in 1998 they received a shocking setback when Lieutenant Colonel Watkins was tragically killed by a collapse of clay while accessing another tunnel system beneath Vimy Ridge. Twentieth century battlefields are intrinsically difficult and dangerous places to work, and those of the First Wold War particularly so. Not only is the risk of unexploded munitions constant, but often the ground being worked is inherently unstable, shattered through years of shelling. The Durand Group go to great lengths to ensure that all projects are conducted in as safe a manner as possible and that all risks are minimised, but all members are aware of the hazards.

Lieutenant Colonel Watkins is commemorated by a dignified and fitting memorial in the form of a bronze plaque, erected by Veterans Affairs Canada and located near to the entrance of the Grange subway at Vimy Ridge. After the loss of such a dedicated member of the team it was decided that the best way to honour him was to continue the Group's work, allowing for his vision to be fully realised. Accordingly, the Group has since undertaken a wide variety of projects across the old Western Front, surveying, recording and investigating many different underground features ranging from deep tunnel systems to large souterraines and dugouts, all of which were utilised by the various armies of the war.

It was here that the Durand Group, perhaps unwittingly, embarked on a modern conflict archaeology approach, combining the Group's skills to devise new approaches to the First World War's hidden landscapes. All archaeologists are aware of the contested nature of landscapes, but modern conflict landscapes and those of the First World War are the most contested of all. Different local groups and organizations often claim ownership of these places simultaneously and when the Durand Group's work began there were also several former soldiers from the Great War still alive, which added an extra layer of sensitivity to the Group's work.

Tunnel systems can extend for kilometres and are regularly linked with each other. Their extent often takes them beneath several villages, each of which are governed by local mayors and councils that need to be consulted. Landowners' permission is also required and so any research must acknowledge that the spaces these subterranean artefacts exist in are at the same time; ritual spaces, tourist locations and political entities – not to mention repositories for tonnes of unexploded munitions. They are also sites of national (and personal) pride and heritage. As a result, from the Durand Group's inception, a main concern has been to involve local people as much as possible, allowing for the formation of extensive links across Northern France with landowners, farmers, politicians and archaeologists. Several of the Group's current members are French and live near to the Group's area of operations. These local connections provide invaluable support and along with the Group's professionalism, these approaches have enabled hitherto unprecedented access to some of the most unique parts of the old subterranean frontlines.

Much of the Group's early work took place around Vimy and approximately six kilometres of British and German tunnels were initially explored, including the British La Folie and O Sector, and German T-19 fighting systems. Two further mine charges were diffused including a smaller camouflet charge,[13] and an initial 600 m (1970 ft) of the British Goodman Subway was also excavated. The Group worked closely with the municipality of the nearby town of Arras in investigating the Ronville tunnel system beneath the town and assisting with the exploration

Nick Pryor and Arnaud Durier of the Durand Group in the British La Folie system beneath Vimy Ridge. Space in the system is extremely constricted and a high level of professionalism is required to operate in these environments. (©Author/Durand Group)

of the Wellington Mines, today developed into a subterranean museum. Over the last fifteen years the Group's work on the Somme has excavated a German listening tunnel, Stollen 10C, at Serre, demonstrating how the Germans went to great lengths to protect their own underground defences from the British sappers. German dugout systems at St Pierre Divion and at Beaumont Hamel, along with a German tunnel at Y-Ravine, have all been investigated highlighting how prepared the Germans were for the great July 1916 offensive, and why it was that the so many were to die assaulting their positions. Gaining access to the British First Avenue tunnel allowed for a direct comparison to be made between British and German subterranean systems on the Somme in 1916. The last five years have found the Group working beneath the Loos battlefield, exploring its numerous and extensive systems, carried out with the support of the local authority and the *Association Sur Les Traces de la Grande Guerre*.

All the group's activities and excavations are underpinned by extensive archival research and a variety of non-intrusive techniques have been employed in the course of investigations. Due to the geology of much of the Somme and Artois regions of France geophysical techniques, including Ground Penetrating Radar, Electro Magnetic Induction and Soil Resitivity Surveys, have proved of limited value. However, innovative techniques including drilling and the use of remote cameras on fibre optic cable has proved to be a useful reconnaissance tool. The Group's research projects have exposed the importance of tunnel systems to a wider audience, and served to place the relevance of underground warfare during the conflict in its proper context. This, in turn, has done much to dispel commonly held myths concerning the perceived lack of competence in the way in which the war was conducted, and shown how First World War battlefields were diverse and ambiguous. These places have been revealed as multi-dimensional locations where modern industrial warfare was waged with progressive tactical and technical innovation, extra-ordinary logistical competence, skill, and precision.

Along with fighting tunnel systems the Group has also brought wider attention to the existence of souterraines[14] and the vital role they played during the conflict. These features can be found under much of France's Western Front and were highly sort after by all sides to protect their troops, serve as forward command posts, aid stations and communication and logistic hubs.

Lieutenant Colonel Mike Dolamore and Major Andy Hawkins of the Durand Group in Stollen 10C at Serre on the Somme. The tunnel was likely a listening position, or it was for another purpose and never finished. Only one item of Graffiti was found - dated April 1918. (©Author/Durand Group)

Aidan Clearly of the Durand Group excavating a German dugout at St Pierre Divion on the Somme. The remains of several beds were found, demonstrating how effectively men could be housed underground on the front line. (©**Author/Durand Group**)

The knowledge subsequently gained from these large subterranean spaces has contributed to a reassessment of the relationship soldiers shared with the earth, and highlighted the extent and intimacy of this partnership. Many tunnels, particularly the subways, contain a significant concentration of graffiti and intricate carvings – material culture from the war that has revealed much concerning the life, experience and thoughts of the soldiers. Yet it is the souterraines that have concealed and protected the greatest quantity of this very personal material culture.

Nowhere is this better demonstrated than at Maison Blanche, a modest-sized souterraine near the village of Neuville St Vaast. While the Durand Group's research in Maison Blanche is covered in more detail Chapter 5, it is nevertheless true that these hidden worlds are providing archaeological and anthropological data that cannot be found anywhere else on the old frontlines. The eclectic mix of the Group's expert members fosters an inter-disciplinary environment, and one that is able to go far beyond the constraints of military history and battlefield archaeology. Long periods of time spent in souterraines like Maison Blanche or in deeper tunnel systems elsewhere on the front has allowed for a personal perspective to be applied to these subterranean landscapes. The result has been a greater appreciation of what it was like to be in these stifling places during war, producing an anthropological perspective that is not possible without a personal interaction with these cramped and airless locations.

Replicating war conditions exactly is not possible, of course, yet because these environments have changed so little since the conflict the physical experience of being in them today is not totally dissimilar to the experience of the First World War soldier. This is particularly so with the souterraines further behind the line where the immediate danger was not as pressing as in the deeper fighting systems. Perhaps the most intense experience of being in these underground places is the sheer sensuality of engaging with such alien environments. The way the earth feels, the taste of chalk dust in the air, the manner in which sound travels, the way the body is forced into unnatural positions, feelings of claustrophobia and sensorial confusion, a lack of oxygen and the way in which a lack of light marginalises vision are all insightful findings that contribute to the experience.

The Durand Group's multimedia dissemination of their extraordinary work has allowed some relatives of those who fought in the war to visit these subterranean spaces to witness their ancestors' traces carved or written on the walls. The importance and relevance of the Group's research has been showcased too in academic research.[15] Members of the Group continue to advise on the underground features at Vimy and training is provided for the many young guides who work patrolling the memorial site to inform visitors of what they see. A section of the Grange Subway has been preserved and made suitable for visitors, and it is the centrepiece of the battlefield experience at Vimy. Although the accessible section of the Subway is relatively close to the surface and has a good ceiling height, Grange is connected to the deeper La Folie fighting system, where the landscape is very different. As part of their basic induction, new guides are usually taken through one of the gated spurs leading off the main tunnel and down into the deeper system. By escorting the guides to the head of a deep sap they are able to better understand how the Grange Subway is only part of a much bigger integrated system – information that often proves valuable in answering questions from wide-eyed tourists!

The following case studies of Loos and Vimy incorporate much of the Group's work, and this insight, along with the dedicated, professional and academic approach of the Durand Group, has allowed for these battlefields to be reappraised, which in turn is enabling a wider appreciation of the conflict on and below the Western Front.

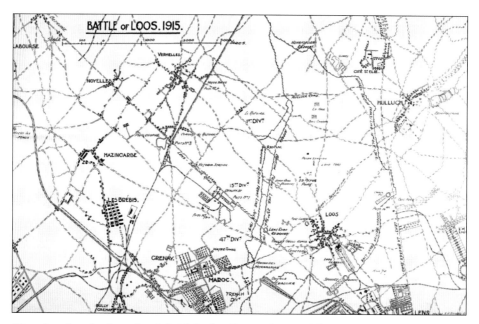

Map showing the Loos battlefield during September and October 1915 (© **Public Domain**)

Chapter 4

The Hidden Battlefield of Loos

One hundred kilometres south of Ypres' waterlogged battlefields are Thiepval, Beaumont Hamel and Albert, nestled in the rolling chalk hills of the Somme. So notorious are these places that, more often than not, they dominate the British understanding of the First World War. Between these infamous locations is the Artois, a sprawling area of industrialised countryside, where the geology changes from the clays of Belgian Flanders to the chalk of the French equivalent. Stretching from Armentieres in the north to Arras in the south, the Artois has become a forgotten, almost mythical site of 'French' failures, 'Canadian' victories and the infamous Battle of Loos, where the British lost any innocence they still had by late 1915. Of course the failures were not just French nor were the victories solely Canadian – the current incarnation of the Western Front tends to portray a nationalised history of the war.

Captain A. C. Morris of 3rd Australian Tunnelling Company standing near an entrance to Hythe Tunnel in a communication trench known as Hythe Alley, near Hill 70, Loos. **(© Public Domain)**

At first glance, around the old coal-mining town of Lens and its suburb of Loos-en-Gohelle (Loos), the war's myriad legacies appear less obvious than on the Somme or around Ypres. Cemeteries and memorials are fewer in number and less grandiose, tour busses visit less frequently and the tourist 'landscape layer' draped over so much of the Western Front is barely perceptible. In part this is because only one major battle was fought in the area between 1914 and 1918, one in which the British suffered heavily. It is also because Loos shares the Artois battle-zone with Vimy, site of the famous Allied victory during 1917. The Vimy Memorial Park is one of the most popular destinations on the Western Front, and it draws visitors away from Loos' less dramatic landscape.

Nevertheless, surrounding the town lies an entire, and almost untouched, battlefield, comprising bunkers, dugouts and complex tunnel systems. On the surface redoubts and mine craters mostly hidden in small copses that puncture the crop-laden fields, hint at what lies beneath, and the number of unmarked graves in the cemeteries tell of the brutality of the war in this area. Once the events of September and October 1915 were over, the construction of the subterranean battlefield accelerated here, and for the remainder of the war little fighting took place on the surface. Below the story was very different.

Under the southern outskirts of Loos still lies the British 'Copse' system of

Copse is a complex multi-level tunnel system comprising elements of subway, listening and fighting tunnel. (©**Author/Durand Group**)

tunnels (so called as it lies beneath the old Chalk Pit Copse of the same name), a complex and dynamic landscape, multi-layered, ambiguous and still lethal. In 2010 the Durand Group began risky but cutting edge research at Copse, elements of which are explored later in this chapter. These tunnel systems offer a chance to get closer to the archaeology of the conflict, to stand and crouch in the same space as the men who made them, to feel something of what they felt, to hear as they did, and to touch and taste the musty remains of their subterranean war. The human senses are powerful constructors of place, and the modern archaeological-anthropological techniques applied to the study of Loos' Copse system would reveal much about the everyday life of these underground warriors.

Loos shares the Artois region with the heights of Vimy Ridge (see Chapter 5) an imposing physical obstacle barely 15 km (9 miles) south of Loos itself. The Ridge was in German hands for most of the war, glowering over the Douai Plain to the northeast, and the outskirts of the Labyrinth to the southwest – an area so-named because the war had turned it into a warren of tunnels, trenches, mine craters, destroyed villages and hamlets, connected cellars and souterraines. The Labyrinth was fought over throughout the war, first by the French during 1915 and then by the British after the French had moved to Verdun. While in British hands the tunnelling companies were kept busy expanding souterraines and constructing tunnel systems in preparation for the Battle of Arras in 1917, of which the attack on the German positions at Vimy played a major part.

The Durand Group has worked around Vimy for fifteen years, excavating subways, dugouts and souterraines, most notably the Goodman Subway on Vimy Ridge and the Maison Blanche souterraine near the village of Neuville St Vaast. Both are discussed in Chapter 5. At Loos, the majority of the subterranean landscape was created after the eponymously named battle, precisely because attacking on the surface was so dangerous. At Vimy, the reverse occurred, with tunnels and souterraines created or appropriated to facilitate a major advance above. At Loos the lessons of the underground war were learned. At Vimy, they were put into practice.

Loos – the forgotten battle

On 12 September 1914, less than 50 km (31 miles) from Paris, Germany's dream of a swift victory was annihilated on the banks of the River Marne. The war of movement was exposed as nothing more than a figment of military imagination, and 250,000 German casualties (and a similar number of French) provided a disturbing portent for what was to come. A year later, almost to the day, on 25 September 1915, the British and French launched the Third Battle of the Artois (also known as the Second Battle of Champagne), a combined assault involving a major British attack at Loos, as well as French attacks in the Champagne at

Men of the 47th London Division advance through the British gas cloud on the morning of 25 September 1915. Note how little can be seen by the camera – even less would have been visible through the eyepieces of the rudimentary gas masks the soldiers wore. (© **Public Domain**)

Tahure, La Folie and La Main de Massige, and at Vimy. It all ended in abject failure.

For the French, the battle was a catastrophe. Twenty divisions attacked along a 30 km (19 mile) front, supported by a thousand artillery pieces and a veil of poisoned gas.[1] Not a single *poilu* reached the German second line, and along the entire front of the attack the furthest advance was just 3 km (1.8 miles). For this grand effort the French suffered 143,567 casualties.[2] At Vimy they fared little better.

Foch's 10th Army attacked Vimy's imposing ridge on 26 September 1915, the day after the British attacked at Loos, capturing what was left of the village of Souchez to add to the strategic spur of Lorette taken earlier in the year. Souchez was so badly destroyed during its capture that hardly a building was standing when the French entered the village. And the Germans still held the Ridge. France's disastrous campaigns of 1915 on the Artois, in the Champagne and among the mountains of the Vosges cost her almost 1.5 million casualties.

While the French were hurling themselves at the slopes of Vimy, the British were in the process of their own forlorn hope north of the Ridge at Loos. Since the defeat on the Marne the Germans had been busy solidifying their positions, and all along the front, wherever possible, the high ground had been captured, reinforced and secured. At Loos, German forces had constructed a formidable defensive line up to 5 km (3 miles) in depth, with concrete machine gun posts covering the space between two defensive lines. The slag from Loos' coalmines formed tall crassiers (man-made hills) several metres high, ideal for use as machine gun nests and artillery observation platforms. Deep bunkers and well-prepared trenches had also been constructed within and around them, hidden from the British. Formidable defensive positions at the Hohenzollern Redoubt, the Dump and Mad Point protected the Germans where No Man's Land had shrunk to little more than a few hundred metres wide. Further aiding the Germans, delay after delay occurred in the build up to the battle as the British assembled more and more artillery pieces, infantry units were bolstered and preparatory assault trenches were dug. All in full view of the defenders. The British were doomed.

Not only had the Germans plenty of time to prepare, they had also positioned much of their artillery and reserves on reverse slopes replicating the Duke of Wellington's manoeuvre a century before at Waterloo. British counter-battery fire would therefore be largely ineffective and the German artillery could shell the British with impunity as they formed up to attack, before switching to No Man's Land, turning it into an inferno of high explosive and molten iron once the assault troops advanced.

Before the battle both the British and the Germans had been at work beneath the surface in the Loos/Lens sector, but this activity was a mere taster of what would follow. During October 1914 both sides had begun digging beneath the outskirts of Cuinchy, south of the La Bassée Canal, and the sector was particularly hated by both the British and German infantry due to the increasingly regular mine detonations. Come September 1915, this cratered landscape would severely hamper the right flank of 2nd Division's advance, forcing the assault troops to meander their way across No Man's Land, desperately trying to find a way through the cavernous craters.[3]

Pre-September 1915, mining had also been carried out at the nearby 'Brickstacks' (an area used to stack great piles of bricks from a pre-war factory) where from April 1915, 170 Tunnelling Company had been waging a hidden war against the German pioneers. Here too the effects of the subsurface detonations would hamper the British during September 1915, forcing elements of the Staffordshire Regiment to pick their way between the old craters, all the while under relentless fire from German machine guns sited in the individual stacks of brick.[4] Underground activity had therefore already played a role on the Loos battlefield before September 1915, destroying much of the fledgling, invisible subterranean landscape and simultaneously creating a new cratered one on the surface. In 1915 mining was still in its infancy and the craters were a serious issue for assault troops, forcing them to abandon advancing in waves, even in places along the attack-front where mining had not been so prevalent.[5] At Vimy the following year the lessons learned at Loos concerning these unnecessary mine detonations would be heeded, greatly contributing to the Allied success.

Faced with such obstacles it is perhaps difficult to believe that the Allied Command had any hope of success in September 1915. The aim was to cut Loos off, squeezing the Germans into an indefensible salient from which they would be forced to withdraw. Yet the British had not yet conducted a serious offensive, and were naïve to the consequences of attacking entrenched positions across such shattered ground. It didn't matter, the pressure on the French, who had been doing most of the dying, simply had to be relieved. The same applied to the Russians, who were being comprehensively beaten on the Eastern Front and were in danger of collapse. The British efforts at Loos then were part of a wider battle plan, but even so, General Haig, Commander of the British 1st Army, had serious reservations about the ground to be covered, which offered very little in the way of cover.

Despite the reservations, it was not all bad news from the British Command's perspective. They had a manpower superiority of 7-1 and Haig intended to attack across a short front, enabling him to focus all of his firepower onto a small area. To prepare the ground ahead, 250,000 shells rained down on the Germans over the four days preceding the attack (a pitiful number by later standards[6]), and at dawn on the 25 September, 140 tons of chlorine gas was released from hidden canisters. It quickly caught the breeze and drifted forward, followed by a fighting force of six divisions advancing towards the German trenches, and on into the unknown.

Three of these divisions were regular army – the 1st, 2nd and 7th – and they attacked alongside the 9th and 15th, both Scottish New Army divisions. The sixth was the 47th London Territorial Division. In reserve were five divisions of cavalry waiting to exploit any breakthrough. Closer to the action waited the 21st Division, 24th Division and the Guards Division, which would be required to move forward once the initial assault waves had engaged. This, like almost every aspect of the battle did not go according to plan. Firstly, the breeze soon died, allowing the gas to sink into the shell holes of No Man's Land, and then slowly retreat back towards the British lines. Soon after the killing began.

The gas release had been disastrous, and within minutes almost 3,000 British troops became casualties of their own High Command's tactics, as chlorine filled their lungs. For those clambering out of the trenches, over the writhing bodies of their gassed comrades, the visceral experience of this new type of warfare proved to be a terrible assault on the senses. Labouring under the load of their equipment and the weight of their fear, the soldiers advanced into a sensorial No Man's Land. The noise was violent and overwhelming, shouts and screams mixed with the crack of bullets and crump of heavier rounds. The gas reduced visibility to little more than a metre, and the misted-up eyepieces in the crude gas masks made things even worse. These cumbersome devices, meant to protect the men once they reached the German lines, were already starting to fail before the men had left their own trenches, and some removed them, only to fall into the churning morass of fire, mud, gas and death, gasping for breath and clawing at their throats.

The use of poisonous gas and the wearing of gas masks in combat were important elements to the sensorial experience of the First World War soldier. Sight was severely restricted, and the sense of smell corrupted, especially by the first crude masks that were often little more than a handkerchief or rag soaked with urine. In any type of mask breathing became difficult, especially when running, and the types of material used and the closeness of the fit formed further haptic engagements with the body. The French soldier André Pézard wrote of how some men could not stand the experience:

> There are the guys who go crazy, who take out the cannula to call for their mothers. They swallow the poison gas, they begin to cough, to spit, to vomit up their guts. They run for the door, they howl, they demolish the partitions by hitting them with the pumps or with their heads, until we go and collect them.[7]

The attack continued regardless, and the German machine guns were soon decimating the advancing British lines. In front of Hohenzollern Redoubt the carnage was terrible, yet somehow the outer defences were still breached. The 7th and 9th Divisions clung on in the face of overwhelming fire, but they couldn't hold out indefinitely. Elsewhere, continual shelling from the supporting German redoubts made things as bad along most of the northern sector of the advance. In some places it was much worse. Astride the La Bassée Canal 2nd Division were savaged and failed to achieve a single one of their objectives.

Further south things appeared more hopeful and positive gains were made towards the village of Loos and onto the slopes of Hill 70, but they too were to be short lived. The reserve divisions had not moved forward when the battle began, causing them to arrive too late to be effective. In the face of innumerable and savage German counter-attacks, the British were slowly pushed back from their foothold on Hill 70. The Germans, unlike their enemy, quickly filled the gaps in their lines with fresh reserves. The first day had not gone according to the British plan and some 8,500 of their soldiers lay dead or dying. On the second day things would get much worse.

As night fell on the first evening, the British reeled from their mauling and prepared for the following morning's offensive. The Germans rushed forward as many men as possible, reinforcing their already formidable positions. On all sides soldiers steadied themselves for what was to come, each preparing his body and mind in readiness for the forthcoming barrage of corporeal chaos. It was a cold and damp night and despite the exhaustion few could sleep. Those holding captured German positions grasped the full extent of what awaited them the following day. Far from the defences being shattered by the bombardment, most were still in serviceable condition, something highlighted in a report from some men of the Guards Division that spent the following night in a captured dugout on the Grenay Ridge:

Both officers and men were filled with admiration at the intricate dugouts they found, twenty to thirty feet down in the chalk; evidently great trouble had been expended on this part of the line, and the German officers had been accustomed to live almost in luxury.[8]

The attack was renewed at 11:30 on the second day. The 21st and 24th Divisions, who had arrived late the previous night, formed up with the Guards Division and marched rapidly to the village of Sailly les Bourses, where no sooner had they arrived they were ordered forward again to their jumping off positions. They were to attack the German second line. Both the 21st and the 24th Divisions were untested in battle and could not have imagined what lay ahead. Even the Guards contained its fair share of raw recruits. Most, having marched all night, were soaked through, shivering and exhausted. There was little food and water, and even less time in which to consume it. These new divisions along with the Guards, left their trenches in good order, and advanced with only limited artillery support. The German second line was beyond the effective range of the British 18-pounder artillery, which had been unable to move forward during the night over the ruptured ground of the first day's attack. Instead of advancing on smashed German positions, they walked into the teeth of the enemy's re-supplied guns, into a world they did not understand, bombarded mentally and physically, and were annihilated.

As confusion reigned in the British ranks, the Germans were dumbfounded at the brazen audacity and raw courage of their attackers. Many even climbed out of their trenches to pour fire onto the British assault waves – one machine gun alone fired over 12,500 rounds that afternoon.[9] So great was the carnage that eventually the Germans stopped firing, unable to bring themselves to kill anymore of their enemy. The decimated British were allowed to retreat unmolested back across the corpse-ridden field of Loos, where at least 8,000 of their number lay dead or wounded. Over the next three weeks of fruitless attacks they were to be joined by many more. So terrible was the slaughter that only 2,000 of those killed on the opening day have a known grave, the rest are still missing. As the battle drew to a close, a thin strip of violently contested land only 3 km (1.8 miles) deep had been gained for a total British cost of 16,000 dead and over 25,000 wounded. For now, there would be no more grand British attacks across the killing field of Loos.

The aftermath: going underground

A unique aspect of the Loos battlefield was that there was a pre-existing subterranean landscape there before 1915. The Lens/Bethune area had been a coal mining area since the nineteenth century[10] and several collieries (known as fosses) could be seen on the Loos front in 1914. These fosses were accompanied by small groups of miner's cottages, pithead towers and crassiers that had been well fortified by the Germans. Chief amongst these was Fosse 8, which along with its assorted small buildings and a 6 m (18 ft) high slagheap, known as 'the Dump', presented a formidable obstacle to be overcome by the British in 1915.

Despite the presence of this underground labyrinth, the coalmines were not fully developed by either the French during the initial months, or the Germans and British for the rest of the war. Before 1914, shafts had been positioned to provide multiple entrances and exits from the coal mining system, and this meant that once the war came to Loos on either side of the front lines the same coalmines could be accessed. Ernst Junger wrote of how these mines were a confusing labyrinth to the Germans, who without any maps (which were all in French possession) blundered around in the dark trying to make sense of the maze.[11] The atmosphere in the coalmines was deeply oppressive. They were hot, the air was bad and they were so vast that it was almost impossible to traverse them without getting lost. Additionally, the German explorers continually ran into their French opponents and there were many instances of hand-to-hand fighting in the pitch black depths.[12]

Despite not being developed for defensive purposes, from late 1914 the coal galleries were used as a conduit for spies on both sides, enabling them to cross

Loos was a coal mining area before 1914 and many of the fosse (pit heads) *dotted the battlefield. Both sides shelled them and the mines were flooded with gas and then blocked off, rendering them all but unusable. (© Public Domain)*

beneath the lines in relative secrecy.[13] Incredibly, it suited all to leave these clandestine passageways open. In July 1915 Second Lieutenant Dixon and a small group from 170 Tunnelling Company managed to use the coalmine passageways to gain access to the bottom of Fosse 8, which was behind enemy lines. Their mission was not to put a stop to the spying or to gain access to the German tunnels but rather to establish whether or not the Germans could flood the mines and therefore affect the British ability to tunnel effectively in the area.[14] Dixon reported that the Fosse 8 shaft was blocked with debris and that it was of no use to either side – the risk of being flooded underground seemed to be mitigated

The Germans, wary of the French and then the British being able to access their lines through the mines, attempted to saturate the system with gas whenever possible, and each shaft behind their lines was filled with debris ranging from spoil to corpses.[15] The British, with help from the French, blocked many of the passageways, rendering the mines almost impossible to work in. There was no ventilation and once the majority of the shafts had been blocked, it left a subterranean world full of noxious gasses where no one could survive. Each side would have to be content with creating their own new subterranean system, and both the British and the Germans did just that for the rest of the war, deep beneath the terrible battlefield of 1915.

After the battle both sides realised that a major breakthrough was unlikely to come at Loos, the ground was just too unsuited to massed infantry attacks. Within a few months the Germans would launch a massive strike against the French at Verdun, and during the summer of 1916 the British and French would attack in Picardy, drawing away German reserves from the area. At Loos, it would be a case of holding the line and here the war went almost exclusively underground, with both the British and Germans adopting new versions of old military siege tactics. The subterranean landscape they created required a particular sensorial engagement if it was to be effective as a means of both defence and attack, but despite the connections formed between man and landscape at Loos, the casualty rate beneath the surface was greater than anywhere else on the Western Front. The underground war at Loos was extensive, brutal and total, and today much of this subterranean world still exists, relatively untouched, but still potentially lethal.

Within days of the battle ending 170 Tunnelling Company, under Captain Frank Preedy, began digging beneath the German strongpoint at the Hohenzollern Redoubt. While doing so they discovered that the enemy had done likewise and was already beneath the British trenches.[16] The German offensive tunnels were immediately destroyed and a concerted effort was made to mine the redoubt. Soon the British began to gain the upper hand and in the three months that followed they blew more than fifty mines. Eventually, Preedy's men got beneath the Redoubt and the hated obstacle that had claimed so many lives was charged with three large mines. They were detonated at 5.45pm on 2 March 1916. George

Coppard (who would go on to write *With A Machine Gun To Cambrai*) witnessed the detonations:

> At the moment of explosion the ground trembled violently in a miniature earthquake. Then, like an enormous piecrust rising up, slowly at first, the bulging mass of earth cracked in thousands of fissures. When the vast sticky mass could no longer contain the pressure beneath, the centre burst open, and the energy released carried all before it. Hundreds of tons of earth were hurled skywards to a height of 300 feet or more, many of the lumps of great size.'[17]

Elsewhere in the sector, within weeks of the battle shafts were sunk all along the line from Grenay to the La Bassée canal. From south to north (initially) these mining sectors were called; Double Crassier, Triangle, Copse, Hill 70, Chalk Pit Wood, Hulluch/St Elie, Quarries, Hairpin, Hohenzollern, Cambrin and Cuinchy. By the war's end the result was a vast underground web of tunnels and dugouts, a subterranean landscape that became home to thousands of men, all of whom had to renegotiate their relationship with the world in order to exist beneath the surface. Charles Bean, the Official Australian Historian of the Great War, remarked of the area:

The Hohenzollern Redoubt seen today. This was a formidable German defensive position in 1915 consisting of machine nests, barbed wire obstacles, mantraps, supporting trenches and dug outs. (©**Durand Group**)

To the north of Lens near Hulluch, where I went through the workings with Sanderson, the whole defence of the front appears to be underground. The infantry garrison lives underground, trench mortars and their crews are underground. The machine guns are underground and for a mile behind the front line the communication trenches are underground. The light railway delivers stores to the gun emplacements by an even lighter railway – underground![18]

The year of 1916 was one of massed pitch battles that raged elsewhere along the front, while the fighting at Loos remained hidden. The situation remained much the same until the Battle of Arras began in April 1917. Initial British successes during that battle forced the front lines forward around Loos, constricting the German's there into an exposed salient. By May, they had retired from their positions on the southern edge of Loos (the village had remained in British hands after the 1915 battle) to reserve lines around Hill 70.

On 15 August 1917, Canadian Corps launched an assault on Hill 70, and the northern outskirts of the city of Lens. They managed to secure the heights of Hill 70, and then succeeded in drawing the Germans into one counterattack after another, during which the Canadian artillery wrought havoc. In January 1918 Hill 70 was further fortified in preparation for the expected German spring offensive. Old fighting tunnels were converted to subways and new ones were constructed to move men quickly, and in relative safety, along the line. Machine gun posts were installed along with numerous trench mortar batteries as the British replicated the scale and depth of the German defences they had faced in 1915. This time it would be the Germans that would have to run the gauntlet of massed defensive fire.

In the event, the German attack did not come in any strength around Loos. They may have been confident in their huge assault on the Allied lines, but the memories of so many British dead only a few years before still burned bright in the German memory. They had no wish to suffer the same fate. An unsuccessful raid was made to regain Hohenzollern Redoubt, but little else, and the anti-tank defences laid by the British between Chalk Pit Wood and Hulluch proved redundant. By the middle of 1918 the Loos battlefield was even more unsuited to a surface attack than it had been in 1915, and the area remained a backwater until the Allied advances of August 1918.

The Copse British tunnel system

In 2010 the Durand Group began exploring the subterranean world of war beneath Loos. This meant entering British and German underground features and multi-layered tunnel systems, most notably the British 'Copse' fighting system.

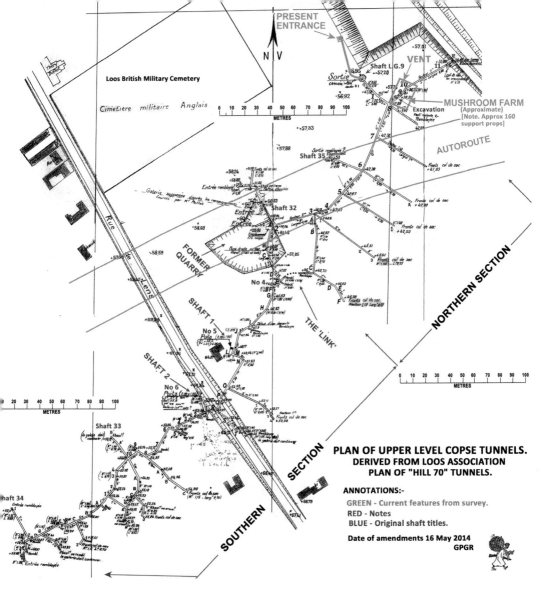

Map showing the extent of the upper level of the British Copse tunnel system at Loos-en-Gohelle. (© **Durand Group**)

Copse is located on the southern edge of Loos-en-Gohelle and has three levels, comprising listening and fighting tunnels, subways and possible mine charges, as well as a narrow gauge railway. There are few direct references to Copse in post-war literature on the underground war, although it is mentioned briefly in *Crumps and Camouflets: Australian Tunnelling Companies on the Western Front*[12], 'Only days before the battle, [of Arras in April 1917] the company's mining front had been extended to include the British mining system known as the Copse'.[19]

Despite the dearth of references in the published literature, it is mentioned in various unpublished Tunnelling Company war diaries, such as this one from 13 January 1916:

> A preliminary inspection of the Copse area proved the enemy to be within blowing distance of our front line:- a shaft No 9 was therefore started in the nearest and deepest dugout in the vicinity and sinking was begun on top of the German gallery on 13.1.16. The company also took over the Double Crassier mining sector (about 2,000 yd to the west) and the Hill 70 sector to the east of the Copse.[20]

It is perhaps the sheer extent of tunnelling at Loos that explains the lack of written evidence. Subterranean activity was so extensive that soldiers referred to the myriad systems under the pejorative term 'the Loos tunnels' as opposed to by their direct names – something that was not unusual along most of the front.[21] This highlights how fighting tunnel systems were a widespread and intrinsic part of trench warfare, and were therefore not seen as unique by those occupying the front lines.

The British and Dominion Tunnelling Companies were not the first to operate in the area and 173 Company's war diary refers to existing French galleries (tunnels) in January 1916. Old tunnels would regularly be recycled and incorporated into new systems – a practice that contributed to the cultural construction of these spaces, and also one that enriches the biography of many subterranean landscapes.

173 Tunnelling Company suffered terribly during their time in the Copse sector. 45 men were killed, along with a further 46 from the attached infantry during May 1916.[22] On 4 April 1917, just prior to the Battle of Arras, the 3rd Australian Tunnelling Company took over the sector. They faced a No Man's Land in front of the Copse, which, 'like other intensely mined areas of the front, was characterised by a series of large conjoined mine craters, dramatic scars in the landscape from the earlier mining battles waged against the underlying mine systems.'[23]

A war diary entry for 18 April mentions how the Company salvaged timber from the British and German mines at the Copse, indicating that the Germans had recently withdrawn from their positions both at Copse and Crassier.[24] At the end of the month another entry records, 'With this month ended the mining work in an offensive and offensive-defensive way. The enemy ceased mining, evidently realising, as had been proved time and again, that our miners and mining methods were far superior to his own'.[25] The reality was somewhat less heroic. Despite the competence of the British tunnelling companies, the Germans had only withdrawn as part of a wider plan to consolidate their positions, re-establishing their defences further east beneath the slopes of Hill 70. They had certainly not lost the stomach for fighting underground.

Between May and July, 3rd Australian Tunnelling Company maintained and manned listening posts, constructed communications trenches, dugouts and battle headquarters, and continued salvage work. One of the brigade headquarters they constructed was at the Quarry, where work was started on or about 19 July. An entry in the war diary states: 'Work Completed at the Quarry Bde HQ. Chambers of old mine gallery and re-timbered gallery M6c.90.30. Bunks installed with timber salvaged from old enemy galleries'.[26] The Canadian Corps attacked the nearby Hill 70 on 15 August 1917, with the 3rd Australian Tunnelling Company remaining in support. From this point onwards, offensive work declined and from January 1918 the Company, along with 1st Canadian Tunnelling Company, were involved in creating the nearby Hythe and Canteen subways and linking these to existing tunnel systems.

After the war, sometime during 1919, the tunnel entrances in the Loos sector were systematically filled in. A few of them, however, remained accessible and locals used part of the system for storage. At some point during 1944, access was again facilitated to Copse by American forces, this time from a previously closed entrance in a nearby quarry. The quarry was later filled in when the A21 Autoroute was constructed, leaving only one remaining entrance to the system; an incline near the British Commonwealth War Graves Commission cemetery at

Durand Group member Tony Edwards inspects the shattered remains of the Quarry HQ in the Copse system. It was likely destroyed by collapse or possibly with a camouflet charge. (©Author/Durand Group)

Loos. It appears the tunnels were initially of little local historical interest, and instead a large space was excavated at the bottom of the main incline for use as a mushroom farm, which once completed was almost immediately abandoned due to the excavated chamber's instability.

Interest was piqued in the tunnel complex when the mushroom farm was abandoned and members of the local mining community attempted to open up the system in order to take tourists along the left-hand section of tunnels, which had been developed towards the end of the Great War as a subway for the movement of troops. A local organisation, the *Association Sur les Traces de la Grand Guerre,* used this section of tunnel for this purpose until 1998, at which point access was prohibited by the local authority on health and safety grounds. Although only the initial part of the subway was used for these tours (a section of around 50 m (145 ft) in length) the absence of a secondary entrance and exit was given as the main safety problem. The *Association* requested the Durand Group conduct a safety inspection and the same conclusion was reached.

Visitor access was suspended in 1998, although members of the *Association* and the Durand Group have entered the system since then, and a BBC film crew were accompanied into Copse by the Durand Group for *The One Show* in May 2014, allowing the international public a rare glimpse into a First World War subterranean landscape. One of the few available published sources for the Copse System is a small article by Robin Sanderson, which appeared in *Trust News Australia* during February 2012.[27] Robin is the grandson of Major Alexander Sanderson DSO, MC and Bar, the Operational Commander of 3rd Australian Tunnelling Company who first conceived connecting the Hythe Tunnel to the Copse system in 1918. Sanderson has accompanied members of the Durand Group into Copse on several occasions, forging a generational link between this subterranean landscape, a century-old war, and the present day.

Restricted access to Copse has had its advantages – helping to preserve much of the system's graffiti as well as the overall structural integrity of the tunnels. Nevertheless, constant vibrations from A21 traffic and natural erosion from water ingress and animal burrows have caused minor collapses, and some artefacts have been damaged or lost. Consequently, the archaeological recording of the system and its contents has been a priority for Durand Group researchers.

The excavation and exploration of Copse was a major undertaking demanding that several experienced teams work together, often far from the surface. Safety was (and always is) of paramount importance. The system has three levels: Main, Deep and Deep Deep, and although the Main level was mostly collapsed; the Deep and Deep Deep levels were accessed in their entirety. The southern section of Copse's Main level consists partly of a subway, and partly of narrower fighting tunnels, which include listening posts and temporary accommodation for the tunnellers. The smaller dimensions of the southern section make it more claustrophobic still, and most of it has to be arduously crawled along. The mundane struggling along these smaller sections of tunnel generated a strange kind of empathy between Group members and those who had done the same 100 years before. Often there was water underfoot (and knee!), helmets clanged off the low ceiling, hands grasped for the chalk walls and breathing became laboured.

Some 270 m (885 ft) from the entrance, the Main level provides access to the Deep Deep section via a narrow shaft that descends vertically for almost 22 m (72 ft). Over the years the ceiling had collapsed, filling the bottom of the constricted shaft, and so entering the Deep Deep was a considerable engineering challenge. Nick Pryor, the Project Manager, and one of the Group's founder members, devised a system of removable ladders and fixed platforms installed at 3 m (9 ft) intervals, which allowed for excavated spoil to be removed from the shaft. The operation involved a two-man team filling buckets with chalk debris – sometimes mixed with live grenades – which were then winched up for disposal. This was hazardous work, oxygen levels were often poor and the danger of further collapse was ever present. The teams were regularly rotated, but the environment was oppressive – working in a shaft 30 m (98 ft) below the surface, in a space only 2 m², and these conditions required a level of professionalism and experience unique to the Durand Group.

At such depths even minor accidents or injuries can pose a serious threat, and a major injury much worse. To prepare for such an event, the Group practiced safety drills underground. Major Andy Hawkins 'volunteered' and was lowered to the bottom of the shaft to play the part of an injured team member. The rest of the team practised how a casualty would be removed, which involved

To reach the Deep Deep section a system of platforms and moveable ladders was devised allowing for safe access. Working conditions in the shaft were oppressive, oxygen levels were low and the dangers of falling or collapse were ever present. **(©Author/Durand Group)**

winching the patient up the shaft and then laying him out on a stretcher that could be dragged along the tunnel floor. The casualty was then assessed by Dr Arnaud Durier, a Group member and trauma specialist, and then evacuated from the system on the stretcher. This was no easy task, and it took a ten-man team over four hours to get the casualty clear of the tunnels. Professionalism, adequate safety measures, the presence of a doctor and the ability for teams underground to work together efficiently are an essential element of subterranean research.

With the shaft cleared, access was gained to the deepest part of the Copse system. This level had remained sealed since the war's end in 1918. A century-old time capsule, it had preserved the remains of a light railway, and 14 side tunnels, some probably listening galleries, others blocked and maybe harbouring volatile high explosives.

Durand Group member Aidan Cleary in the Deep Deep level. The level consisted of listening tunnels, a light railway and possible tamped mine charges. Levels of preservation were good and clear imprints of hobnail boots were recorded. (©Author/Durand Group)

First World War tunnels do not usually contain large amounts of war detritus

The Deep Deep level contained a light railway that had remained largely in tact. This was used to transport spoil from digging as well as explosives and supplies for the tunnellers. Small turntables were used at junctions to change the direction of travel. (©Author/Durand Group)

The Copse system contains various artefacts. The pick seen here was likely used in the system, but the Livens Projector may well have been placed there by the Association Sur les Traces de la Grand Guerre. **(©Author/Durand Group)**

and materiel, and Copse was no exception. Raw materials such as wood and metal were highly valued during the war and were soon removed and repurposed once the tunnels had fallen out of use. However, the narrow gauge railway was in remarkable condition and small arms ammunition, in the form of .303 cartridges, was frequently found throughout the system along with mess tins, picks, and more fragile items, such as pieces of webbing, and the remains of boots and uniforms.

Graffiti survives throughout the system, especially in the eastern subway. Most is Canadian, but British examples are present, presumably from infantry who worked alongside the tunnellers, as labour or security. One notable piece was a caricature of Kaiser Wilhelm II, which stands out for its political tone, something not often found in British graffiti. Another appears to be German and was discovered above the entrance to the shaft. It is highly unlikely that any Germans entered these particular tunnels during the First World War, so it was possibly (and interestingly) written during the German occupation of France during the Second World War, although there is no proof of this. Likewise, examples of American graffiti are found in the southern section of the system, with dates revealing a definite Second World War origin. Candle soot has been used to write names and initials in some places, and probable First World War candle stubs are still in situ on many walls.

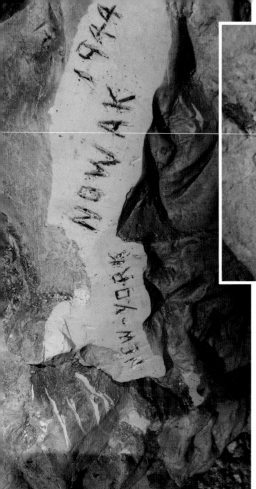

The 2nd Durham Light Infantry were one of the British units that occupied Copse. As well as graffiti from other infantry units, several tunnellers have also left their marks. (© Author/Durand Group)

US servicemen entered Copse during 1944 as the Allies swept through France. The presence of this Second World War graffiti adds an extra 'layer' to Copse's biography, demonstrating how modern conflict landscapes are often recycled. (©Author/Durand Group)

Aside from personal graffiti, there are several instances of official wartime written instructions. They are of particular interest, offering an insight into how these landscapes were constructed, as well as how those that occupied them orientated themselves in such an ambiguous environment. Messages were left for men taking over digging work so instructions could be passed without the need to speak, thereby minimising sound. These are mostly located at tunnel junctions, or right angle turns and usually at eye height, complying with the somatic understanding of these landscapes – searching for instructions in a dark and confined space was unnecessarily time-consuming.

Other objects demonstrate the sensorial realities of working underground. Sound, both its creation and detection, was a major part of life, and one of several listening tunnels has a carved-chalk bench at the end, designed to ease the burden of long and mentally tiring shifts. Listening tunnels are an integral and distinctive physical feature of the subterranean conflict landscape and have a powerful sensorial dimension. Those tasked with detecting an approaching enemy were usually alone, in candlelight, their body and mind as in tune as possible with their material surroundings. Both sides were constantly listening

Leaving instructions written on the walls minimised the need to talk. Silence was paramount in front line tunnels. Throughout the system are several of these types of messages. Tunnellers could never be sure how far away the enemy was. (©**Author/ Durand Group**)

for the other, and at strategic locations instructions were left to this effect. Personal graffiti allows for some former occupants to be traced, forming a direct link between individuals and landscape, and instructions provide an important research tool for understanding life underground – messages 'to listen' highlight how important it was to keep completely silent with the unseen enemy so close by.

Engaging life beneath Loos

The Durand Group's work at Copse has exposed the physicality of a First World War multiuse tunnel system, greatly adding to the archaeological-anthropological record and furthering our understanding of the subterranean war. A decade ago the dimensions, layout and mapping of Copse would have been considered enough, but modern approaches to the archaeology of twentieth century conflict can deliver far more. A nuanced and intimate study of how the human senses engaged with and helped to create this landscape, and how this in turn affected the minds and bodies of the soldiers and tunnellers themselves can now be explored.

Tunnel systems were intrinsic to trench warfare and were thus landscapes truly in flux. Copse contains subway, fighting, listening and headquarters features and the system adapted to changing demands and functions as the war progressed. Subterranean warfare under the Loos battlefield was intense, requiring that those who fought there well understood the environments on which their lives depended.

Although no other systems in the immediate region of Copse have been fully surveyed, the Hill 70 and Hythe systems are in close proximity. The entire area was heavily mined and the proliferation of listening tunnels and possible mine chambers at Copse, particularly in the Deep Deep section, as well as war diary entries, suggest that German tunnels were close by. This made Copse a sensorially demanding environment perhaps more suited to the tunnellers than the infantry.

Tunnellers were mainly (but not exclusively) recruited from civilian 'clay-kickers'[28] used to digging narrow tunnels for pipe work and cables, and mineral miners or diggers accustomed to working in confined conditions, usually in coalmines, sewers or on the construction of subterranean railways. Nevertheless, the working conditions beneath the Western Front threatened far more dangers than either group were used to – controlling or reconfiguring the senses was vital to deal with these risks, especially in the more complex subterranean landscapes. The High Command had its doubts as to whether even the clay-kickers could adapt to the conditions. Even for the most experienced miners the assault on the senses began almost as soon as they were recruited.

> It was argued, justly, that ordinary miners would adapt themselves to the different working conditions. This, however, was no easy task – particularly under the deplorable conditions prevailing at the front, but the men faced it gallantly and successfully. Theirs was no pleasant initiation – a hurried call from civilian work, a scramble into uniform, a Channel crossing which almost took the heart out of them, followed by an appalling rail journey in cattle trucks. Then, within a few hours of reaching the battle area, with not the slightest allowance for acclimatization, they would find themselves underground.[29]

Tunnellers worked with infantry whenever they were underground, who offered protection from attacks and helped with the removal of spoil and carrying of equipment and explosives. The infantry had little or no experience of working so deep beneath the surface, initially leaving them at more of a disadvantage than the tunnellers, but for both the realignment of the senses required to work in such close aural proximity with the enemy was a skill that had to be learned as the numerous references to 'being quiet' or 'listen here' found on the walls of Copse emphasize. Deep fighting systems were dangerously ambiguous environments; and shafts and tunnels were named or numbered in order to mitigate the problems

As well as minimising noise, both sides were constantly listening for the other. The message left at this location indicates that the German Pioneers were likely near by.
(© **Author/Durand Group**)

of moving through them quickly and safely. Under the pressure of living and working with these subterranean dangers, a distinctive vocabulary developed (transmitted through whispers, touch and signage), forming a direct link between language, landscape and those who occupied these spaces.

Keeping noise to an absolute minimum underground was a life-saving habit quickly acquired. On the surface noise was commonplace, if not overwhelming. Yet underground, in dugouts or deeper fighting tunnels, silence reigned. If even the faintest tapping noise of enemy diggers was heard it meant potential danger, and when the digging noises stopped, men's nerves became strained, as they waited for what might come next:

> The bravest men, who never funked a "show" which involved hand-to-hand fighting, have confessed to nervous fears as they have crouched in a dugout listening to the monotonous tapping of enemy miners below. So long as the tapping continued there was safety – it was the occasional silences that were terrifying, then the enemy might be charging his mine – at any moment might come death in its most horrible form. Our infantry had stood the strain of that appalling first winter of the war – deficient in numbers, with utterly inadequate trench equipment, they had held their own against a courageous and persistent enemy. Now a new trial oppressed their harassed nerves; above, death came suddenly; below, his approach was slow and stealthy, and the waiting time was enough to shake the stoutest heart.[30]

Re-evaluating the importance of sound was not the only realignment of the senses required in the deeper fighting tunnel systems. Clay kickers and miners were used to confined spaces, but at the front they often worked in very poor light, forcing them to operate by sensing with their bodies rather than by sight. Used to digging through soft clay, the harder chalk provided an altogether different feel for the 'kickers', and was difficult to excavate using the same methods. This required a change of body position and a re-learning of muscle memory.

Adding to the cramped discomfort, the dust emitted from the chalk quickly smothered everything, making breathing laboured and affecting taste and smell. The lack of oxygen seriously compounded this problem, but there were often other gasses present in larger volumes than would be the norm on the surface. Chlorine and mustard gas could seep down into tunnel systems, either through the chalk or via inclines and shafts, so gas doors were fitted at the top and bottom of entrances. However, the real danger to those underground was carbon monoxide gas, released when mine charges were detonated. Carbon monoxide is invisible and undetectable by the human senses, and it claimed the lives of many underground. Specialised units using breathing equipment known as 'proto sets' were trained to rescue those who fell victim to the silent killer, and canaries or mice were regularly taken below ground, their deaths acting as an early warning system. In addition, gas doors were placed throughout tunnel systems. These were usually wooden frames cemented into the tunnel walls, with a leather curtain

that could be rolled down to block the spread of the toxic vapours, and there are several present throughout the Copse system.

At Loos those digging into the crassiers experienced abnormal changes in temperature, which only served to increase the suffocating feeling of being underground. There was a geological issue as well, inasmuch as the slag that formed these man-made spoil heaps retained its

One of the many gas doors found throughout Copse. The leather curtain has long since rotted away, but the wooden frame remains largely in tact. Note the way that bricks have been added to the top of the frame. It was imperative that gas doors formed a perfect seal, preventing noxious gasses from passing through the system. (©Author/Durand Group)

heat from the mining process, often for years. The temperature underground in chalk tends to stay at a steady 11-12° Celsius, providing a reasonable working environment. In and beneath the crassiers the temperature could be much higher, causing tunnellers and their infantry support to sweat profusely, have difficulty breathing in the hot air and become dehydrated.[31]

The dimensions of the Loos tunnels were dictated by the military handbook, which instructed fighting tunnels to be dug approximately 0.9 m high x 0.5 m wide (3 x 2 ft), requiring men to crawl, or walk bent double and when two passed each other one would lie flat on the ground and the other scramble over him.[32] This intensified the bodily contact between men heightening the sensorial realities of subterranean landscapes. By the end of 1915, the rigid adherence to these dimensions was beginning to be relaxed, providing better working conditions, and tunnels were expanded up to 1.5 m in height x 1.2 m in width (5 x 4 ft).[33] The subterranean environment was still highly restrictive but the confined space allowed men to more easily touch the walls, ceiling and floor, in effect 'anchoring' them in the dark tunnels. Fighting tunnel systems were meticulously mapped onto paper, allowing soldiers and tunnellers to 'see' their extent. But the tunnels themselves were usually not 'seen' at all; rather they were experienced with the whole body. Understanding this allows for a fuller appreciation of what could be called the existential experience of life underground.

The design of fighting systems such as Copse, as with most military underground features, was dependent on which army created them, but the dimensions, extent, depth and proximity to danger were similar, and so were the methods used to construct them. As the first tunnels in the Loos sector were dug before the end of 1914[34], Loos serves as an excellent example of how the understanding and prosecution of subterranean warfare progressed as the war developed. Many of the lessons learned underground at Loos after the 1915 battle were later applied elsewhere on the front.

Militarily, Copse demonstrates several different features of mining; listening galleries, fighting tunnels, a multi-level system, possible mine charges and a change of use from offensive mining to the underground transport of men and equipment. Yet it also serves as an excellent example of the sensorial realities of living and fighting underground. As so, perhaps, it can also be described as a 'sensescape' as well as a landscape. Conducting research in this environment has enabled a fuller realisation as to the human experience of the war at Loos after the 1915 battle, but the extent of Copse also alludes to the more general experience of being underground across much of the Western Front, highlighting the importance of sensorial interaction in the creation of a new sensecape/landscape.

The investigation of the Copse system forms just one element of the Durand Group's work around Loos. It is part of a larger, and ongoing, project entitled 'Engineering the Loos Salient 2015-2018', which is involving the

Graffiti takes many forms, and this artefact located in the Wings Way Subway near Hulluch is better described as art. Here the artist has created a tunnel within a tunnel, layering landscapes on top of each other. (©**Author/Durand Group**)

local community and authorities to bring the area's Great War life back into the public domain. As well as Copse, the Group have entered several tunnels in the vicinity of Hulluch including Wings Way, Devon, Green Curve and the Stansfield Subway. Work is also continuing around the Hohenzollern Redoubt, and when complete the findings will be published. At the time of writing research is still in its initial stages, but several artefacts of interest have been discovered, including moveable defensive walls that could block off tunnels compromised by the enemy, fascinating graffiti and access to the deeper mining system, which has yet to be fully surveyed. There is also an element of Second World War subterranean landscape at Wings Way. During the latter part of 1939 the Royal Engineers accessed the old Great War system and blocked off some tunnels and created others. When the Germans invaded France in 1940 the speed of their advance was so great that Wings Way was quickly abandoned, leaving a highly ambiguous conflict landscape beneath the 1915 Loos battlefield.

The Durand Group's physical experience of working beneath the Loos battlefield demonstrates how individuals can reorder the way their senses operate in order to more effectively create and navigate space. Even today, with the aid of modern equipment such as Gore-Tex, LED lighting, safety rigs, air monitors and the luxury of not worrying about the possibility of lethal enemy action, these sensorial interactions are very similar to those experienced by tunnellers and soldiers in 1915 and beyond. Space still has to be navigated through an increased awareness of touch, sound travels strangely along passageways, and chalk continues to affect taste and smell.

As the Western Front extended south eastwards from the French and Belgian coasts the geology changed. In Belgian Flanders the earth is mostly clay, a very different medium to tunnel through than chalk. French Flanders and the Artois are mainly chalk, which continues beneath the Somme and on to the Chemin des Dames. As the front lines meander through the Argonne and down towards Verdun the chalk gives way to sandstone, forming a substance known as *gaize*, which is equally suitable for tunnel construction. Towards the Swiss border, the ground rises and becomes harder until eventually it is solid granite, but nevertheless trenches and tunnels were still carved into the rock.

In other theatres of the war, such as the Italian and Austrian Alps, tunnels and trenches were created in glaciers and mountains, forming subterranean landscapes several thousand metres above sea level.[35] Each of these geographical locations

The subterranean landscape around Hulluch is extensive. To facilitate construction and the movement of supplies light railways were used. Many of the sleepers are still in situ, as are several rail carts and turntables. (© **Author/ Durand Group**)

A century after the battle of Loos heavy rainfall has contributed to several collapses in local fields. Here a section of the German second line has revealed itself. The holes are likely the result of collapsed dugouts close to the surface. (© Andy Prada/ Durand Group)

had its own unique sensorial attributes on the surface, but the experience of being underground was similar along all fronts of the war. For the Allies, the soggy clays of Belgian Flanders were kept at bay underground with wooden boarding and metal braces, though the Germans commonly boarded all their tunnels and dugouts regardless of geology. Likewise, tarpaper was regularly used by all sides to 'wallpaper' their dugouts. The British would wood-line chalk tunnels when raw materials were available, but the New Zealand tunnellers preferred to leave their systems bare whenever possible, arguing that the 'earth spoke to those that could understand its language'.[36]

These similarities in the corporeal understanding of life below ground mean that the experience of being in one system can be extrapolated to another. Tunnellers and soldiers may have worked in different mediums, but sight remained compromised, sound was of upmost importance, and touch became a prime means of navigating the underground world. Even the chalk dust beneath Loos and the mud below Ypres equally determined the power of taste and smell. While the war continued at Loos almost unseen from the surface, on the nearby Vimy Ridge the British were busy underground for an entirely different purpose.

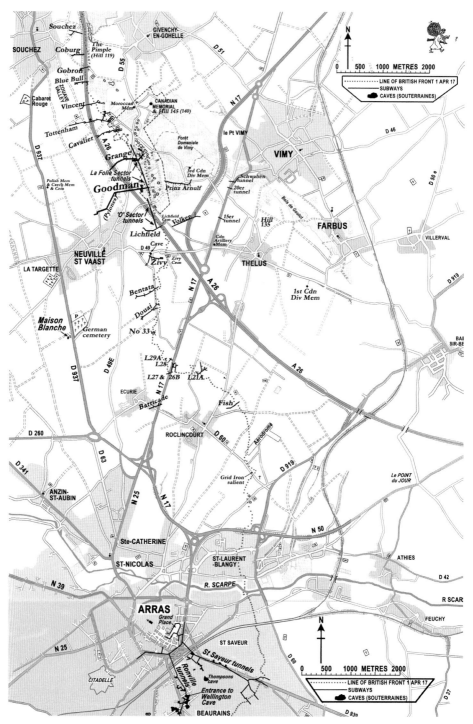

Map of the Vimy battlefield in 1917. (© **PGR Robinson**)

Chapter 5
Vimy and the Labyrinth

For the next three years, many lessons were learned beneath the corpse fields of Loos, often at terrible cost, but the knowledge gained was put to good use elsewhere on the front. 1917 saw the Battle of Messines shatter the German positions around Ypres with the detonation of nineteen enormous mines, the subterranean infrastructure for which had been carefully laid down over the preceding two years. At Vimy, the year would witness another devastating demonstration of how far British tunnelling companies, and the ability to co-operate with other forces had come. On the 9 April, as part of the larger Battle of Arras (itself a part of the Second Battle of the Aisne) the Canadian Corps of First Army and XVII Corps of Third Army would storm the heights of Vimy, finally knocking the Germans from the high ground and into flight across the Douai plain.

The Vimy sector has proved fertile ground for Durand Group research since 2000, revealing much about the way the subterranean war was waged in this area. On the Ridge itself, three tunnel complexes were investigated – the German

This entrance to the Goodman Subway is located within a section of the Vimy Memorial site closed to the public. Originally a trench would have housed this shaft. The Durand Group constructed the present entrance to the Subway. It can also be accessed via the La Folie system. (© Author)

T-19, and La Folie and O Sector, the British counterparts. All have provided a great deal of information about how subterranean life at this part of the front was lived, how close the two sides were underground, how nationalities differed in constructing their subterranean systems, and the manner in which mine detonations were used to achieve various ends.

The Goodman Subway was another underground system targeted by the Durand Group. It was one of at least twelve along the Northern heights of the Vimy Ridge (some subways joined), and was one of the vital arteries constructed for the 9 April 1917 attacks on the First Army front. The Durand Group's investigations here demonstrated the importance of these features, showing how they were used in conjunction with souterraines and the wider trench network above. The research has also provided a raw, unaltered and authentic comparison to the sanitised and publically accessible Grange Subway in the Vimy Memorial Park.

Just 5 km (3 miles) to the southeast of Vimy the Maison Blanche souterraine has around a thousand examples of graffiti on its walls, all of which have been painstakingly recorded by the Durand Group. The Maison Blanche images reveal personal attitudes towards the conflict, army life, national pride and the realities of being in an industrial war.

The battles that raged in this part of the Artois, along with their subterranean elements are dealt with extensively elsewhere.[1] Here, my aim is to demonstrate how the underground landscape developed around Vimy, altering the fabric of the battlefield, and the lives of those that occupied it. As this chapter will explore, the La Folie system shows how the British were able to gain the upper hand on the Ridge, developing an effective defence against the German tunnellers before finally achieving superiority. Without this subterranean superiority the Goodman Subway could not have existed, as least to the same degree of effectiveness, and the use of souterraines to protect men prior to and during the battle for Vimy Ridge would have become redundant if soldiers had to leave the protection of the earth to attack on the surface. Together, these underground features form a convenient symmetry, which will be discussed in this chapter from an archaeological and anthropological perspective, allowing for a holistic overview of the fighting around Vimy, and thereby providing an opportunity to better understand the life of a soldier on this part of the front.

The 'Vimy' battles of 1914 and 1915

Before the British took over the Allied positions on Vimy Ridge in early 1916, it was an exclusively French and German battlefield, and one that witnessed some of the war's bloodiest early clashes. In the final months of 1914, with their Schlieffen Plan in tatters after the defeat on the Marne, the Germans began to consolidate the ground they held right across the front. Even though both sides attempted to outflank each other in the so called Race to the Sea, Germany was at the same time unwilling to give up any of the territory it held, and accordingly embarked on an ambitious project to make its defensive lines impregnable to the Allied attacks that would inevitably follow in the spring. At Vimy, by December 1914, the Germans had control of the Ridge as well as the tactically important villages of Carency, Neuville St Vaast, Souchez and Ablain-St-Nazaire. Additionally they also controlled the Lorrette Heights, which provided added protection for the rich coal fields of the Douai Plain on which Germany so heavily relied.[2] Facing them were the French, who knew that any attempt to take the Ridge would require Lorrette and the surrounding villages to be taken first. This was the aim of the approaching battle.

Before the bloodletting of 1914 could be stemmed, the French assaulted Carency in an attempt to get the upper hand, in what became known as the First Battle of the Artois. It failed, but the French continued to launch attack after attack on the German positions until they were ruthlessly counter attacked during March 1915. Within hours the Germans had taken back the small area of land the French had managed to conquer, and although by the end of the fighting the French had retaken it, the cost of 3,300 casualties was a price too high to pay. It was during these attacks that the French first employed mines to attack the Germans[3], a portent for what was to come at Vimy.

The Second Battle of the Artois began on 9 May 1915 and within three days a foothold had been gained at Lorette, although it would not be secure until the end of the month. Despite this success, the villages around Lorette were ground to dust, and Vimy Ridge itself refused to fall. Nevertheless it was a victory of sorts, at a stage in the war where victories were in short supply, especially for the French. In much of the fighting it was France's Colonial troops who had the success, and did most of the dying.

On the first day of the battle the French African Moroccan Division, in what was a superhuman feat of arms, managed to break through to the German positions on the peak of Vimy Ridge. The gallant attack is described by Henri Barbusse in his seminal war novel, *Le Feu* (*Under Fire*) as 'one of the finest of this war or any other'. As the whistles blew, the Africans charged headlong across what later became known in their honour as the 'Zouvae Valley' and took their objective. Despite this courageous act, their efforts were unsupported and they soon found themselves at the mercy of the enemy guns, their bright red fezzes doing little to camouflage them amongst what was left of the verdant Artois fields. The attack faltered. Denied support and reinforcements, the Moroccans were cut to pieces and six months later many were still rotting on the enemy wire, their bright red trousers fluttering in the breeze.[4] The Zouave's valiant effort is memorialised today on the Moroccan Memorial near the modern car park on the summit of the Ridge.

By the time the battle ended on the 18 June the French had paid dearly for their efforts to take Vimy Ridge. Some 102,000 men were dead, dying, wounded or captured. Nevertheless the French policy of '*attaque a outrance*' *(attack to excess!)* ensured that soldiers were forced to make frontal assaults on deeply entrenched positions time and again. Within eighteen months, French regiments at Verdun would bleat like sheep as they went into battle, and in 1917 the army mutinied. Enough was enough.

Despite the failure of the Second Battle of the Artois three months later the French renewed their efforts, this time in conjunction with the British at Loos. Again, the losses were terrifying, and again the Ridge was not wholly taken. Nevertheless, the villages of Ablain-St-Nazaire, Carency and Souchez did fall, allowing the French to push the Germans back to the very edge of the high ground, meaning they were no longer able to defend in depth. This kick-started the underground war with renewed intensity and the Germans quickly constructed an impressive series of tunnels and subterranean features to support their counter attacks which pushed the French part way back off the high ground.

During the Artois offensives of 1914 and 1915 the destruction of the landscape mirrored the trauma suffered by the soldiers. Henri Barbusse served at Vimy during the Third Battle of the Artois, and witnessed the destruction first hand. In *Le Feu* he describes the devastation through the eyes of Poterloo, a soldier who before the war had lived his whole life in the village of Souchez. So terrible is the destruction that when Poterloo ventures back to Souchez once the Chasseurs (French cavalry) had retaken it. What he finds is nothing like he remembers:

> The village has disappeared. Never have I seen such a disappearance of a village. Ablain-Saint-Nazaire and Carency still preserved some semblance of locality, with their gutted and truncated houses and their courtyards filled with plaster and tiles. Here, framed by the shredded trees – which, in the midst of the fog, surround us with a ghostly sort of décor – nothing has any shape; there is not even a fragment of wall or railing or gate still standing, and we are amazed to discover, under the heap of beams, stones and ironmongery, that there are paving stones – here used to be a street![5]

The confused and broken Poterloo cannot even identify the house he has lived in for most of his life such is the utter destruction, It's there – no, I've passed it. It's not here. I don't know where it is… where it was… Oh, misery![6] Barbusse fuses landscape and soldiers, describing how each destroyed the other as the violence escalated. Souchez and Poterloo become indistinguishable from each other, the fate of each framed by the oblivion of endless mud, utter destruction and the hopelessness of war. Nowhere around Vimy was this fusion of man and nature more apparent than in the area known as the Labyrinth.

The Labyrinth

If the French were ever going to capture the Vimy heights then the area to the immediate west of the Ridge had to be secured first. This would allow for the necessary resupply of any attempt on the Ridge by providing a sizeable storage area, transport hub, safe inclines for tunnelling, and a relatively secure location for the heavy artillery that would pound the enemy defences on Hill 145 into submission. The Germans, having being in situ since the end of 1914, were well aware of this too, and tenaciously defended every inch of land. The fighting grew in intensity during the second half of 1915 eventually turning the landscape into a maze of trenches, shell holes and mine craters. It became known as the Labyrinth – a place where men could disappear into the ferocious, churning mire of exploding shells and metallic air, never to be seen again. Writing after the war, Captain Plummer of 185 Tunnelling Company described the area thus,

> … such a maze of trenches was The Labyrinth in the old days. When one realises that on our Company's front alone in that sector there were over 100 mine craters and that there were said to be something like 60,000 unburied dead – French and German – lying in No Man's Land, and in shell holes in and around the trenches of the Labyrinth it will be realised that the change in the countryside is remarkable.[7]

The full extent of the Labyrinth is difficult to assess particularly as this entire section of front was so heavily fought over. However, it can generally be identified as the area between Neuville St Vaast and Rolincourt. In these villages archetypal trench warfare became street fighting, with bitter clashes taking place in buildings, cellars and even attics. The Germans had tunnelled between many of the cellars, linking them together into a formidable defensive network. Barricades were erected in the streets, both sides occupied the same buildings and as the village was mercilessly pounded by French artillery, many Germans sought refuge in a large souterraine known as the *Neuville-Grotte*, which shook from the shelling and eventually became the place of nightmares as the wounded poured in, forcing the Germans to evacuate them under the cover of darkness. The space they vacated was soon occupied again.

In an area so consumed by heavy shelling any underground space became a vital refuge. In the immediate area of Neuville St Vaast there are at least eight souterraines used during the war. Some were bitterly contested and at the *Aux Rietz* souterraine beneath the La Targette crossroads, and just across from a large French cemetery, the walls still bear the scars of grenade fragments and bullet holes. Eventually Neuville St Vaast fell to General Mangin's army on 9 June 1915, although much of the Labyrinth remained in German hands as the French, despite firing over 300,000 shells in a 48 hour period just a week later, could not compete with the German heavy guns raining down accurate fire from the Vimy heights.

The French efforts to take Vimy during 1915 may have fallen short, but they did lay the foundations for the eventual removal of the Germans from the Ridge in 1917. In part this was because of the recovery of Neuville St Vaast and a sizeable chunk of the Labyrinth. Nevertheless, the French were to play no part in the eventual capture of the Ridge. In February 1916, General Erich Von Falkenhayn unleashed the Crown Prince's 5th Army at Verdun, sparking what was to become the bloodiest battle of the war, and arguably the bloodiest battle in the history of warfare, which will be explored in the following chapter. Accordingly the French were steadily withdrawn from the Ridge and replaced by British forces, and later in 1916 the Canadians joined them. By now the German underground defences on the Ridge were already considerable, and the French attempts to counter the threat were woeful. The tunnels were too shallow, not extensive enough and suffered from a lack of defensive structure. As the British 3rd Army replaced the French during March, tunnelling companies were rushed to the Ridge to improve the situation. First on the scene were 182 and 176 Tunnelling Companies, swiftly followed by 172, 175, 181, 185 and the New Zealand Engineers Tunnelling Company. By the end of May there were seven tunnelling companies along the whole Ridge, and at last the German dominance of the Vimy heights began to be countered.

Gaining the advantage

After the terrible casualties of 1915, it was clear to the British that if an attack was to be successful, then the tunnelling companies would have to play a major role. Not only would a way have to be found to halt and then reverse the German superiority underground, but also any attack on the German positions would need to minimise casualties. As soon as the British took over from the Verdun-bound French, work began in earnest.

The first task was to create a subterranean defensive line to protect the Allied trenches from attack. Ideally, there should have been three lines of defence, but in reality there was nothing like it. The French gains of 1915 on the Ridge, little as they were, had been trumpeted loudly in France, a rallying call to her allies. When the British took over the sector they realised that not only were the defensive lines in a mess, but the French 'gains' had not been as extensive as had been claimed. The Germans held most of the Ridge and almost all of the high ground, and the French, now British, lines merely clung to the lower slopes. [8]

Undeterred, the British went to work, and harassed the German lines relentlessly. On the surface trench raids became a regular occurrence, a practice that unnerved the enemy, but almost always resulted in friendly casualties too.

Many despised these trench raids, but nevertheless they were an extremely effective way of taking prisoners, discovering opposing troop strengths and most important of all to the Tunnelling Companies, locating the position of enemy gallery inclines. Laterals were dug parallel to and beneath the British lines, ensuring that the Germans would no longer be able to attack underground with impunity. From these laterals the British were then able to tunnel out into No Man's Land and harry the German lines.

The British mining efforts were relentless and although the Germans tried to stem the tide, the regular detonation of camouflet charges did little to deter the British. Huge craters given names like 'Football', 'Love' and 'Irish' began to appear on the surface as the British remorselessly attacked the German flanks.[9] The only respite for the Germans came when they attacked the British lines on the surface, and on 20 May 1916 they launched a major attack on the London Division holding the lines in the Berthonval sector driving them back down from the former French positions near the crest. This managed to halt the British mining, but only for a matter of days – for the British tunnellers now had the upper hand.

A large part of the Memorial Park is closed to the public and still contains original trenches, shell holes and large mine craters. It is part of the Zone Rouge and will likely remain off limits to the public forever. (© **Author**)

The negative effect the British tunnellers were having on the Germans cannot be underestimated. For the best part of two years their positions at Vimy had been relatively secure, and they certainly had the measure of the French engineers underground. Now, the tables were being turned. The British were digging faster and deeper, and the laterals were proving to be a major obstacle. Before long the effect on German morale was palpable, 'Our companies had suffered heavy losses through the British mines... we could not fight against the enemy any longer with his own weapons, for he was superior to us in men and material.'[10] Likewise, a report from the 163rd Regiment stated that, 'The continual mine explosions in the end got on the nerves of the men. One stood in the front line defenceless and powerless against these fearful mine explosions.'[11]

Preparing the underground

As soon as the British took on the Vimy sector of the line they set about countering the German advances underground, and nowhere is British success in this matter better displayed than at the La Folie system. This subterranean complex consists of more than 3 km (1.8 miles) of tunnels incorporating a 1 km long lateral, seven entrances accessed from the contemporary trenches, listening posts and fighting galleries located between 18 and 30 m (60 – 100 ft) below the surface, as well as large mine charges, smaller camouflet charges, and internal stairways.[12] The La Folie system protected the British lines from the opposing German Arnaulf North mining sector, itself a complex of deep tunnels although mostly lacking interconnection with a defensive lateral.

The La Folie system today sits beneath the Canadian Memorial Park at Vimy Ridge. Part of the publically accessible Grange Subway connects to the La Folie system, and visitors are offered a brief glimpse down an incline into the fighting tunnels, but the mine craters on the surface adequately narrate the effectiveness of the deep lateral. Because the system lies beneath the Memorial Park it has been protected and preserved, and therefore still contains many items of material culture (including the aforementioned mines) ranging from gas doors (and even the remains of leather blankets these incorporated), to air pipes, assorted ordnance, seismomicrophones and other listening equipment, as well as several items of carving and graffiti.

Today there are two accessible entrances to the La Folie system, one from the aforementioned sap off the Grange Subway, and the other further to the south in the Goodman Subway. Traversing the system between the two entrances is an arduous task as for much of its length the tunnel's height prohibits walking. In the summer of 2015 the Durand Group entered the system with a Canadian film crew, which served the dual purpose of being able to examine the system for deterioration since the last visit a decade before. The depth of the system makes for slow progress. Oxygen can be limited in places and at points along the route the tunnel becomes very constricted and water levels can reach around 30 cm (1 ft), further reducing available space and air.

So undisturbed is the system that it provides a unique opportunity for phenomenological study, as does the Copse system at Loos. There was no electrical lighting in La Folie, though there was in the connecting subways, and this paucity of light demonstrated the marginalisation of sight and the simultaneous promotion of touch. Even with modern LED lighting equipment, a haptic engagement becomes essential as the tunnel floors are uneven, chalk slabs have fallen from the roof and tunnels are all constricted. Being able to feel through the feet becomes essential when traversing these tunnels. The restricted height means that helmeted heads constantly knock against the tunnel roof causing not only discomfort but also a distraction from the uneven floor. Without the feet's

This sap connects the La Folie system to the Grange Subway. La Folie contains several mine charges, all of which have been rendered inert, but the explosives remain in place. (© **Author/Durand Group**)

ability to interrogate the ground balance would be difficult – and a broken or badly twisted ankle so far underground would make a medical evacuation fraught with difficulty. Without touch taking the lead in guiding the body through this environment, progress would be slow at best and often practically impossible.

Taste is also affected as the fine chalk dust coats the lips and lines the throat. It also gives drinking water a metallic taste, which adds to the general discomfort of these subterranean spaces. The sense of smell remains largely unused, and during our recent archaeological surveys sound also appeared unimportant. Nevertheless, this was not the case during 1916 and 1917, when an acute appreciation of noise was a prerequisite to survival, and along the system's length there are various items of material culture that confirm this. The remains of a light railway were discovered along the lateral. The tracks were wooden and the wheels of the small trolleys were rubber, both materials employed to reduce noise. Listening galleries are evident along the entire length of the system, further reinforcing the importance of sound.

During a Durand Group survey of the La Folie system, a small team entered the opposing German T19 tunnel system, giving access to a subterranean stretch of the German line that came extremely close to the British system, missing it by being 3 m (9 ft) beneath it. So close were the tunnels that the two survey teams were able to sing to each other through the chalk walls. A live 800lb camouflet charge, primed and ready, was discovered at this point in the British system. It remained that way until Group member Lieutenant Colonel Mike Dolamore defused it in 1999. Next to the camouflet was a crude listening device and a clip of ammunition. Together these artefacts offered an extraordinary glimpse into

This camouflet charge has been rendered inert but the explosive ammonal remains in situ. Next to it can be seen a crude listening device made from a section of air hose and a biscuit tin lid. Although the device was never fired, the presence of the listening device indicates that the enemy was close by. (© **Author/Durand Group**)

life below Vimy Ridge during the months leading up to the 1917 attack, and at the same time showed the importance of sound detection in preserving the environment. It was apparent in the German system opposite that they too had detected the noise made by the British so close by. Clearly fearing a break in, stick grenades were found wedged into the walls in anticipation. The connection to the rest of the German system had also been disguised by the construction of a wall across the main tunnel that was in danger of being compromised. So good was this ruse that it was only discovered by accident during the Durand Group's initial surveys.

The La Folie system ably demonstrates the way in which human senses were reconfigured underground, a realisation backed up by many artefacts found along its length. The effects of sensory deprivation however were not so obvious. The loss of sensorial control is not something experienced by everyone who encounters these spaces, and so becomes a personal event, and difficult to document unless it is personally encountered. During filming for the 2015 documentary one of the film crew, who had experience of being underground, and had shown no adverse reaction in other subterranean systems, suffered a panic attack while inspecting the camouflet charge and listening device. Access to the charge is gained by crawling along a very narrow and low-level passage, and this is where the crewmember suffered a sudden and intense sensorial deprivation. While he was quickly able to recover, such an event here in 1916 or 1917 could have been fatal. When sensorial deprivation occurs the mind is unable to keep the body quiet. Involuntary speech, movement and a lack of awareness manifest themselves quickly. The sensorial awareness displayed by those in these deep fighting systems during the war went far beyond a renegotiation of the senses, it also required an absolute control over them.

Digging and arming the La Folie system was a dramatic preparation for the 1917 attacks. The construction of these deep laterals forward of the British trench lines ensured that the Germans were unable to get through the subterranean defences. The laterals were so deep that to get beneath them the Germans were forced in many places to dig into the water table, which caused many problems not least the necessity for almost constant pumping – an impossible situation which denied further advances to the British lines. With German progress stalled, the British were able to construct fighting galleries out from the lateral at numerous places, forcing the Germans to go on the defensive. This had a two-pronged effect. First, it allowed the British to finally gain the initiative, but more importantly it allowed them to construct subways, which in turn could be connected to the souterraines around Neuville St Vaast. Together these would

The remains of a gas curtain in the La Folie system. The studs and straps indicate how it would have been affixed to the wooden frame. (© **Author/Durand Group**)

enable the attacking British and Canadian forces to reach their jumping off points in relative safety. The lessons of Loos and the Somme had been learned, and the mistakes would not be repeated at Vimy.

The souterraines

By the beginning of 1917 war violence had reached its zenith. The battles of Verdun and the Somme the previous year had accounted for well over a million casualties, and it was the artillery that was doing the most damage. Much of the fighting at Verdun represented an artillery duel, and many of those killed and injured at the Somme on the morning of the 1 July 1916 were victims of heavy shelling. Here, as soon as the first attacks went in the German gunners began to carpet the Allied reserve lines with gas, shrapnel rounds and high explosive. There was no protection for these units and the failure to adequately foresee the German response to such a massed British attack was catastrophic. So was the lack of awareness as to how the work of the engineers could be combined with that of the infantry units. Despite the appalling consequences of the 1916 Somme offensive for the April 1917 attacks a serious effort was made to rectify these bloody mistakes.

The use of souterraines to shelter men before and during battles was common practice on all sides by the middle of 1917, and during preparations for the assault on Vimy Ridge several more were brought into service by the Allies. One of these was the Maison Blanche souterraine, located approximately 1.5 km (0.9 miles) south of the village of Neuville St Vaast along the D937 to Arras.[13] It was one of at least eight souterraines which lay to the immediate west of Vimy Ridge and to the south of Notre Dame De Lorette that were used during the War. Maison Blanche lay quietly behind the German lines until the French pushed them out of the Labyrinth in May 1915 during the Second Battle of the Artois.[14] There is no evidence in the souterraine itself or in available records that the Germans, and later the French, used the souterraine or even knew of its existence.

Military records of Maison Blanche are vague and it is only referred to briefly in a small number of regimental texts, one of which is the Official History of the 15th Battalion CEF (48th Highlanders of Canada), many of whom left traces of their occupation on its the walls:

The men slept in the bad air of the Maison Blanche caves during the day. There were many strange tales told about those caves. One of them would hold an entire battalion and, certainly, they were very old and, perhaps, as the tales went, once sheltered fugitives of the French Revolution and the women and children of Arras during the [Franco-Prussian] war of 1870.[15]

As with many of these subterranean spaces, their exact origins are opaque. It is clear from the *puits* (shafts) that Maison Blanche was once an underground quarry, the chalk from which was likely used to build the nearby village of Neuville St Vaast. Until the First World War there is no official record of this, yet carvings and markings found there by the Durand Group indicate that it is likely older than 1870. In 1917, Maison Blanche was one of at least five souterraines used by the Canadian Corps for the attack at Vimy; the others were the nearby Zivy cave and three others located in Zouave Valley, all of which were connected to the Tottenham Subway by 182 Tunnelling Company.[16]

The Zivy cave is fitted out with bunks, tables, cooking stoves, telephones, electric lights, running water and anything else that was essential... The saturated ground above us leaked its moisture through the roof... so there was always an inch or two of greyish white slime underfoot. Scattered about the floor, men could be dimly seen by candlelight, their grotesque shadows dancing on the adjoining walls... Numbers of men with their army clasp knives carved their names and unit numbers on the firm chalk walls... There was a constant

The Maison Blanche souterraine under modern electric lighting. This was installed by the Durand Group to facilitate recording the many pieces of graffiti and carvings that adorn the walls. (© Author/Durand Group)

movement of men entering or leaving the cave. The sound of talking, coughing, spitting and shuffling feet went on without ceasing... The smell of foul air, mud, cooking, sweat, urine, chloride of lime, tobacco and candle smoke filled the atmosphere and was almost overpowering.[17]

Maison Blanche was close enough to the subway entrances on the edge of Neuville St Vaast to be effective as a holding station for troops in reserve, as well as a Battalion HQ.

After the successful Allied attacks on Vimy Ridge in 1917, the Germans retired to the Hindenburg Line, and Maison Blanche fell too far behind the lines to be useful. Graffiti evidence suggests that during the Second World War it was used by refugees and visited by troops, but given the speed of the 1940 German invasion of France it is unlikely it served a military purpose, and there are no records or artefacts so far discovered to suggest that it did so.

Maison Blanche was, at least to some degree, accessible to the public during the inter-war years, and although direct mentions of the souterraine after the First World War are rare, Henry Williamson, the author and old soldier, visited in the late 1920s, remarking,

> Many tunnels here, and of the regimental crests engraved in the chalk maple leaves predominate. The signatures and initials in indelible pencil may have been made yesterday. All drowned far under time.[18]

Williamson also alludes to the fact that others were able to visit the souterraine to see and touch the carvings and graffiti contained within, describing how, 'Candle-flames have smudged the chalk where many curious hands have held them'.[19]

In the years immediately after the war hundreds of thousands visited the Western Front and tour operators focused on especially interesting sites. There is evidence that Maison Blanche was frequented on these battlefield tours, as

Arrows painted on the walls of Maison Blanche are likely from the Thomas Cook tour operator that offered visits to the souterraine during the 1920s. There are many other pieces of graffiti from those who visited, creating an ambiguous archaeological record of visitors to the souterraine. (© **Author/Durand Group**)

the walls of the souterraine carry large arrows painted over the First World War 'archaeological' layer, often with the paint dripping down onto items of graffiti. These arrows were likely painted by Thomas Cook tour guides and were almost certainly used to direct tourists around the souterraine. Similar signage has been found in other subterranean spaces in the area where the tour company was known to operate.

After 1945, the farmer-owner began using the souterraine as a rubbish dump, blocking the small puit and brick staircase entrance, which was not accessed again by the public until 2001. It is not known when the brick staircase was built, but Williamson suggests it was post-war, 'Steps, walls, roof are brick – recently made, for tourists are many, and the dug-out is one of the sights of the battlefields'.[20] That the souterraine remained inaccessible for so long almost certainly had the by-product of protecting it from further damage. As Williamson alludes, visitors were able to touch the walls at will and there are several instances of graffiti left by tourists, something which now forms part of the archaeological palimpsest. In places it also seems likely that some carvings were removed either for sale or personal collections; the sheer number of visitors also contributed to the erosion of the chalk floor and walls.

There is a kind of continuity here today, as private tours can be arranged with the Durand Group and the landowner, but visitors enter at their own risk, and only in small and accompanied groups. Today, the toxic farm waste dumped into the souterraine means that there is currently only one serviceable entrance and exit and clearance would be an expensive undertaking. Drainage is also an issue and the chalk ceiling is in danger of collapse. Heavy rain causes water ingress into the souterraine, further eroding the material culture found within, and at some point the souterraine will collapse in on itself – a fact that lends immediacy to the archaeological recording of the cave and its contents. For all these reasons, it is unlikely that Maison Blanche will ever be fully open to the general public.

The Durand Group have been working at Maison Blanche since October 2006, surveying it, and recording its artefacts in an attempt to better understand its role in the Canadian efforts at Vimy Ridge in 1917. Over 1000 pieces of graffiti have been recorded so far – an extraordinary archaeological record that preserves the traces of many who occupied the souterraine. The emotional intensity of this material culture was vividly demonstrated in 2006 when a Canadian television documentary was made on the souterraine and its graffiti. Working with the Durand Group, the TV production company flew over from Canada Alex Ambler, son of Private A. J. Ambler, who had endured the souterraine in 1917 prior to the Battle of Arras. Private Ambler was a former stonemason, and evidently could not resist leaving his mark as several intricate carvings in the chalk walls. Almost 100 years later, his son created a uniquely personal and sensual link between family, material culture and the subterranean conflict landscapes of a century-

One of Private Ambler's exquisite carvings at Maison Blanche. Ambler was a stonemason before the war and likely brought his tools with him to France.
(© Author/Durand Group)

Alongside the carving opposite, Ambler created a record of his unit's battle honours. Some of the locations mentioned saw very heavy fighting before 1917, which would have prepared the men well for what awaited them on the Vimy Ridge.
(© Author/Durand Group)

old war. All too poignantly, a second visit of Ambler's family was organised for 2007, but Alex was unable to travel, and died shortly afterwards at the age of 93.

Twenty-first century technology caught up with Maison Blanche in 2012, when the Durand Group supported the Canadian syndicate CANADIGM's efforts to digitally map the graffiti and 3D laser scan the carvings with the intention of showing them to Canadian schools and museums. In this way, the lives of an earlier generation of young Canadian men could be experienced through technology with individuals identified from their 100-year-old markings. This innovative project was the first of its kind in Canada, and highlighted the deep cultural significance of the Durand Group's archaeological-anthropological work. Maison Blanche showed without doubt that the subterranean landscapes of the First World War represent some of the last untouched elements of the battlefields and a vital area of modern conflict research.

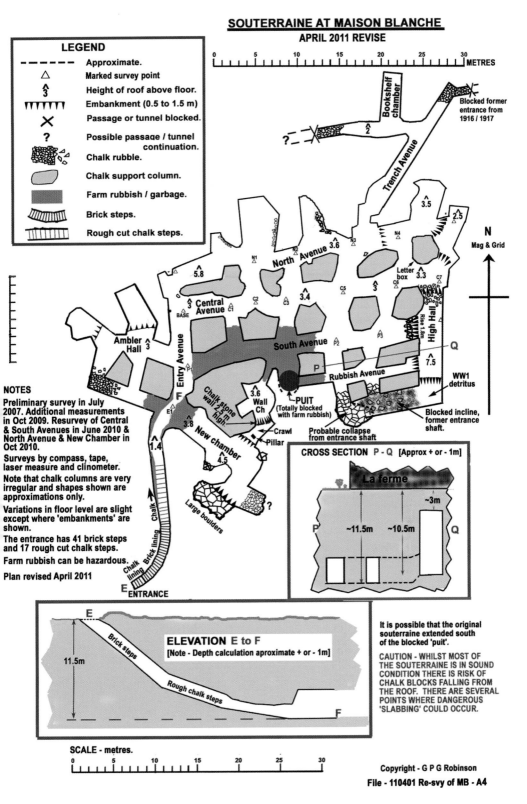

SOUTERRAINE AT MAISON BLANCHE
APRIL 2011 REVISE

LEGEND

– – – – –	Approximate.
△	Marked survey point
↕3	Height of roof above floor.
�	Embankment (0.5 to 1.5 m)
✕	Passage or tunnel blocked.
?	Possible passage / tunnel continuation.
	Chalk rubble.
	Chalk support column.
	Farm rubbish / garbage.
	Brick steps.
	Rough cut chalk steps.

0 5 10 15 20 25 30 METRES

N Mag & Grid

Bookshelf chamber

Blocked former entrance from 1916 / 1917

Trench Avenue

? ✕

↕2

↕3.5

↕2.5

North Avenue ↕3.6

N1 △ 5.8

N2 △

N3 △

N4 △

Letter box ↕3.3

C8 C6

C7 △

Central Avenue ↕3

△ BASE

C1

C2 △

C3 △

↕3.4

C5 △

↕3

High Hall Rise 1.8m

Ambler Hall ↕3

Entry Avenue

South Avenue

P2

P3

Q ↕7.5

WW1 detritus

Blocked incline, former entrance shaft

P1

Rubbish Avenue

PUIT (Totally blocked with farm rubbish)

Probable collapse from entrance shaft

WW1 detritus ←

Chalk stone wall 2.5 m high

↕3.6 Wall Ch

Crawl

Pillar

Large boulders

↕1.4

New chamber ↕4.5

↕3.8

F E1

?

NOTES

Preliminary survey in July 2007. Additional measurements in Oct 2009. Resurvey of Central & South Avenues in June 2010 & North Avenue & New Chamber in Oct 2010.

Surveys by compass, tape, laser measure and clinometer.

Note that chalk columns are very irregular and shapes shown are approximations only.

Variations in floor level are slight except where 'embankments' are shown.

The entrance has 41 brick steps and 17 rough cut chalk steps.

Farm rubbish can be hazardous.

Plan revised April 2011

Chalk lining

Brick lining

Chalk lining

E ENTRANCE

CROSS SECTION P - Q [Approx + or - 1m]

La ferme

~3m

P ~11.5m ~10.5m Q

ELEVATION E to F
[Note - Depth calculation aproximate + or - 1m]

E

Brick steps

11.5m

Rough chalk steps

F

SCALE - metres.

0 5 10 15 20 25 30

It is possible that the original souterraine extended south of the blocked 'puit'.

CAUTION - WHILST MOST OF THE SOUTERRAINE IS IN SOUND CONDITION THERE IS RISK OF CHALK BLOCKS FALLING FROM THE ROOF. THERE ARE SEVERAL POINTS WHERE DANGEROUS 'SLABBING' COULD OCCUR.

Copyright - G P G Robinson

File - 110401 Re-svy of MB - A4

The Durand Group have recorded all the accessible graffiti and carvings in Maison Blanche – approximately 1000 individual artefacts. (© Durand Group)

Today, farm buildings sit directly above the souterraine. The roof of the main chamber is supported by eighteen chalk columns, which along with the walls contain most of the graffiti and carvings. In order to record these each column was given a unique reference and all the avenues and tunnels have been named.

Maison Blanche, like many subterranean spaces created or used during the First World War, contains numerous artefacts of contemporary vintage. Many British Lee Enfield .303 cartridges and several Mills Bomb hand grenades are scattered throughout its underground chambers. Many of these have either been left in situ or safely stored. Besides small arms ammunition and grenades, other discoveries included boots, tin cans, mess tins, bully beef tins, respirator canisters, twisted metal, candles, barbed wire, a trench periscope, and shovels and picks. As the public had previous access to Maison Blanche, many other items could have been removed, but anything of real value would almost certainly been salvaged by Allied forces once the site was no longer required.

The artefacts discovered at Maison Blanche are those commonly found on and beneath First World War battlefields. The war produced this type of matériel on a vast scale, but in archaeological terms these items are almost always found out of context. The battlefields were created and destroyed so often, that no distinct or tidy strata now exist, and at the end of the war much of the surface debris was simply tipped into the open trenches, dugouts and tunnel inclines to facilitate land reclamation, thereby inverting the natural stratigraphic processes. Due to the size of Maison Blanche, and the location of artefacts in relation to former entrances, it is unlikely that all the artefacts discovered there are part of this reclamation process, but it is impossible to tell exactly when they were deposited, and tour companies may even have placed some items in the souterraine deliberately shortly after the war for dramatic effect.

Only two types of artefact retain their original context – the graffiti and carvings that cover the walls. These very personal examples of First World War material culture reveal a great deal about the mindset of those fighting on the front lines.[21] The vast majority of the graffiti and carvings found in Maison Blanche were created by members of the CEF (Canadian Expeditionary Force) in 1917, and as the attestation papers of all those who served in the CEF survive and are available online, these artefacts provide a direct link with the people who occupied the souterraine during the war. People and objects meet underground to produce a complex biography of wartime experiences and their aftermath. Graffiti is found on every wall and pillar, extending vertically to a height of around 4 m (12 ft), indicating that the bunks were almost certainly stacked at least three high.

The record made of the graffiti and carvings is still being collated, but some examples have already been identified and these objects infused with the agency of their creators now stand in for those who occupied this space during the conflict. While it is not the intention to discuss these multi-dimensional inscriptions and their meanings in detail here, three are analysed to highlight the potential these objects have to broaden our understanding of life in the subterranean landscapes of the Western Front. It should also be considered that the inscriptions at Maison Blanche reveal facets of a 'subterranean conflict culture', or what Becker terms a 'culture of war'[22] that existed on the front line.

One of the most prominent carvings is of a letterbox engraved into chalk pillar L.4. The two creators signed and dated their work, and both have been identified from their service records. William Beckett (Service Number 802293) was born on 29 May 1891 in London, England. Having at some point moved to Canada, before the war he was a farm labourer in Kerwood, Ontario, enlisting on 13 December 1915 in Strathroy, Ontario, with the 135th Battalion, transferring to the 134th Battalion on 15 October 1916, and finally to 15th Battalion CEF on 5 December 1916. On 9 April 1917, Beckett took part in the attack on Vimy Ridge and received a gunshot wound to his left arm. Once recovered from his wounds he rejoined 15th Battalion in the field on 7 September 1918. After the war, Beckett returned to Canada on 7 May 1919.

Beckett's co-creator Thomas Mason (Service Number 799610) was born on 23 June 1889 in Cambridge, England. Before the war he was a shoemaker, joining the 134th Battalion in Toronto on 24 January 1916. He subsequently joined the 15th Battalion in the field on 2 November 1916. Mason also took part on the 9 April 1917 attack on Vimy Ridge and was wounded by an explosive bullet

in his right hand, a wound that removed his little finger. He was discharged on 25 August 1917 as being unfit for duty and died on 20 December 1970 at Westminster Hospital, London, Ontario. In one sense, therefore, the letterbox carving is not only a very specific kind of trench art, but probably the last thing which both men would make with their healthy and undamaged bodies, and it is thus a small memorial to their pre-battle unwounded selves.

Carved by Mason and Beckett, this artefact is far more than just a letterbox. It is a direct link to Canada buried deep within the European battlefield. These connections to home were important to young soldiers very far from the world they knew and understood. (© **Author/ Durand Group**)

High up on pillar C1a is a small and unobtrusive piece of graffiti left by William and Clarence Harvey, brothers serving in the Artois district during 1917. Both signed up on 11 March 1916 and at some time before the 4 May the following year they carved their names into the chalk wall. The younger of the two, Clarence, was killed in action on 4 May 1917, so the carving, although undated, represents one of the last times the two brothers were together.

Private Earl Leroy Lacey (Service Number 189458) created perhaps one of the most moving items. He was one of two brothers (and seven sisters) born to a family of farmers at Dunwich, Ontario, on 13 December 1888. Lacey attested on 23 November 1915 with the 91st Battalion and promptly left for France. At some point Lacey was billeted in Maison Blanche and high up on the wall (Location N2) he drew pictures of the animals on his farm at home, creating a direct link with a past he once knew and the landscape of modern war. Lacey was killed on 23 February 1918 while attacking Hill 70 and the Battalion's war diary recounts the circumstances of his death, which was also announced in the *St Thomas Journal* on 21 March 1918:

> …At 5.10 AM party of 10 enemy raided on No. 7 post, right front without success, leaving one dead GERMAN on our parapet. When returning, our wire patrol of 1 NCO and 2 men engaged and fought the party. One of our men, after being wounded, was taken prisoner… our patrols searched No Man's Land for dead enemy without success. Casualties, one wounded (died of wounds).[23]

This small and unobtrusive piece of graffiti high up on a wall of Maison Blanche could well represent the last time the Harvey brothers were together, likely created as they contemplated what awaited them on the heights of the Ridge. (© **Author/ Durand Group**)

Private Lacey did not survive the war, but the record he left at Maison Blanche reminds us that many men were not professional soldiers by trade. They were also young and many would have missed their homes and family. (© **Author/Durand Group**)

In a conflict involving such large numbers of men from so many different nationalities, on a battlefield continually recreated and recycled by industrialised weaponry, these very personal artefacts provide a rich body of material for research by modern conflict archaeologists. Through an analysis of the artefacts it is possible to place individuals within the temporal space of the conflict without the need for service records or war diaries. Maison Blanche is a dynamic subterranean landscape, filled with intensely personal objects of material culture reflecting the experiences of those who occupied this space. As with all modern conflict landscapes, Maison Blanche is a palimpsest, assimilating artefacts, landscape and existential elements, additionally, unless the perspective of sensorial anthropology is applied to the archaeological study of its form, the souterraine's full potential for realising the life of a First World War soldier will remain unfulfilled.

Maison Blanche is just one of many souterraines on the Artois/Vimy front and is therefore not unique. Less than 10 kilometres (3.5 miles) south of Neuville St Vaast is the city of Arras, a city built on top of several large medieval and modern quarries. The cellars beneath the Town Hall and one of the quarries at the nearby Wellington Mines (now a museum) are open to the public, demonstrating how much of war-life in the area was lived underground. These places provide the public a glimpse of the underground landscapes. Graffiti is visible in all these locations and visitors are able to venture underground to get a sense of what life there would once have been like.

'Sense' is a word with many meanings here. The sites open daily to the public are electrically lit and visitors are confined to a strict path. Artefacts are strategically positioned, and in the Wellington Mines video footage, sound effects and imagery all exert their influence. Accordingly, visitors get a sense of what life would have been like without actually using their senses to comprehend the landscape. The eyes are treated to more light than would have been available at the time. Pathways keep bodies and hands away from the chalk walls, restricting touch. Modern ventilation and health and safety ensures that obnoxious smells are kept at bay, something which also ensures that the taste buds are not adversely affected. The soundscape is also strictly controlled so that visitor information can be provided at will. The result is a paradox. The visitor is convinced that he or she can see everything, while feeling almost nothing – the opposite of the contemporary soldier's experience.

The Wellington Mines are part of a much larger subterranean system of quarries and caves that were adapted for war purposes (mainly) by the New Zealand Tunnelling companies. As they enlarged and connected these spaces, they crafted a subterranean map of their homeland. Culturally worlds were being bended together to create new modern conflict landscapes. As individuals left

Lighting has a dramatic effect on how landscapes are interpreted. While recording graffiti it is important to remember that these artefacts were created under a very different sort of light. (© **Author/Durand Group**)

Soot marks on the walls and old candle stubs allow for lighting effects to be replicated, showing how the souterraine would have looked in 1917. The softer light gives a warm aura to the souterraine, making it feel safe and secure.
(© J Richardson/Durand Group)

their marks below ground in the form of graffiti, the New Zealand tunnellers were leaving theirs geographically, crafting landscapes they understood into the fabric of Northern France. A sensual appreciation of subterranean wartime experiences is not part of Arras' underground museum, leaving visitors unaware that they are walking through a world within a world.

The interaction of sight, touch and hearing with the landscape defines space. There is no indication that Maison Blanche was electrically lit, and as there are many soot marks on the walls it can be assumed that candlelight illuminated the entire souterraine. The previous two images show how lighting can affect the understanding of subterranean landscapes. The first image shows Trench Avenue in Maison Blanche lit with modern electric lighting, while the second shows it lit with candles positioned exactly as they would have been in 1917. The character of illumination affected the way that soldiers understood their graffiti and carvings as well as their surroundings, as Henry Williamson noted on his visit to Maison Blanche after the war: 'Down many stairs we reach the caves of chalk. The candle-flames throw a bewildering glimmer in the cold, quiet place. Only the water-drops make a sound'.[24]

Touch is an intimate communicator, and particularly effective at revealing the structure of poorly-lit subterranean landscapes. The chalk walls of Maison

Blanche often feel damp, rough and even sharp, dictating the way that the space is navigated. At its peak, in early 1917, Maison Blanche accommodated several hundred soldiers at a time. The height above ground level at which the graffiti was along with its distribution indicates that the occupants would have slept on bunk beds stacked at least three high. Almost every wall suggests the presence of these beds as witnessed by graffiti or abundant nails likely used to support the bunks. With so many individuals in close proximity the impact of touch on life would have been magnified. Touch allowed for the landscape to be understood in other ways too, as one diary entry referring to Maison Blanche noted:

> Most of the men were on working parties each night, labouring in the front line, supports and in the tunnels being built behind the front line. These, in later days, saved hundreds of men, who sat deep and laughed as concussions shook the shoring and earth trickled down.[25]

These sonic messengers from the surface war reminded the occupants that Maison Blanche was a place of relative safety, despite its dank and oppressive conditions. The smell of food mixed with the less than agreeable aromas of young men at war were exacerbated by the stale unrecycled air in these underground spaces. This in turn affected the sense of taste. Even today, in such underground places, and without the constant wartime vibrations of the earth above, chalk dust quickly fills the air. Water and food carry a hint of chalk and dust coats the lips, and the back of the throat, leaving an unpleasant feeling not present above ground, or in old trench lines.

Souterraines were ambiguous and paradoxical places. They posed a sensual challenge to their temporary inhabitants yet were essential to the Allied plans. Being able to keep large numbers of men safe underground was good for morale and made military sense. With the deep fighting systems on the Ridge now in place, and the souterraines around the edge of Neuville St Vaast adapted and ready to accommodate the troops, the third stage of the subterranean battle plan would be to connect these features together.

The subways

The Goodman Subway, one of twelve[26] on the northern heights of Vimy Ridge, facilitated the movement and support of units attacking German positions on the 9 April 1917. It was fully occupied for the first and only time during the hours before and during the April 1917 attacks. This subterranean landscape, as with the other subways on the Ridge, was ephemeral, fixed in space by time and date, where in the space of a few hours, powerful sensorial experiences between soldiers and their environment took place, and this engagement left a material yet multi-vocal record.

As well as being used for the movement of troops, Goodman also has space for command and control, a reservoir, latrines and cooking. These spaces are linked by smaller side tunnels as seen above. (© **Author/Durand Group**)

The Subway is mentioned in many unpublished war diaries, operational orders and post-war documentation. Goodman was used for 'in' traffic only, apart from runners and officers – a fact not always appreciated. Consequently, no medical attention was available for the wounded inside the Goodman. Those that could make it back to the lines would have had to find another route back to the regimental aid posts at White City Cave and Dowsett Drive.[27]

It was the longest of the subways built for the 9 April attack, constructed 7 m (26 ft) down, and measured 1719.1 m (5640 ft) long, 2 m (6 ft) high and 1 m (3 ft) wide. This was because the ground flattened towards the south of the ridge, so longer subways were required to protect the troops moving forward. Goodman was driven forward from three separate 'faces'[13], the primary one accessed via Albany Trench, the second from a sunken road to the west and the third close to where the tunnel crossed a second sunken road. In December 1916, the already-constructed sections were connected together. Digging speeds varied, but by mid February, the mining report states that 125 m (413 ft) were dug in a single week. In January and February of 1917, the Subway was extended again to the intersection of Pylonnes and Quarries Roads trenches, and at this time a pioneer shaft was dug to meet the Subway and three additional entrances were constructed. By late March 1917, the Subway was largely complete, providing adequate covered approach for the troops that would make the main assault. The stage was set.

In 1989 Lt. Col. Philip Robinson gained access to the Goodman subway via the P.73.J access tunnel – in a section of the Memorial Park closed to the public. Robinson and a team of Royal Engineers (and later with the Durand Group) were able to conduct extensive research over the next seven years. The results of this work are a major contribution to the archaeological record of these First World War landscapes, creating the foundations for further interdisciplinary work to be conducted.

The Goodman Subway contained few artefacts. Grenades and small arms ammunition were found, along with cabling, tools and similar objects. This dearth

Goodman contains several caches of grenades and bullets. Here can be seen still live rifle grenades and .303 ammunition. (© **Author/Durand Group**)

of artefacts is significant and not unexpected for military and cultural reasons. As the subway fell into relative disuse after the April attacks on the Ridge, and was likely not closed off until the 1920s (as with many of the tunnel entrances on the Ridge), there was ample time for post-war souvenir hunters to remove anything of value left by the Army in 1917.[28] Even so, it is unlikely that these trespassers found much of value and equipment and supplies were constantly recycled during the war, so the Army would have removed items of weaponry, ammunition, medical supplies or rations that could be used elsewhere, similar to the case of Copse described in chapter 4. The same applies to raw materials such as wood and metal used in its construction. An understanding of these aspects of military and cultural history informs the archaeological record, explaining why materials were present or absent in the Subway. Modern conflict landscapes are created as much by the removal of items as by their addition.

In this industrial war, military materiel was created on an unprecedented scale, and it is arguable what the discovery of weaponry, clothing or medical supplies in the Subway would have added. But that is not to say that the Goodman didn't offer up some of its secrets. Along the tunnel's entire length graffiti, small carvings and impressive reliefs adorned the walls and columns. The names and numbers of soldiers, regimental badges and short rhymes are written or drawn in trench pencil and ink directly onto the chalk walls, and in some cases the surface had been cleaned or cut flat prior to being so marked. These unique items of material culture range from basic scrawls to fairly elaborate designs, including a maple leaf (which now only partially survives).

The 4th Canadian Mounted Regiment (4CMR) appears to have left the most graffiti (although statistical analysis is ongoing). The regiment was part of the first wave of attacks on 9 April, but also spent considerable time in the tunnel after the battle. Much of the Goodman graffiti probably relates to men who would see action on the morning of the 9 April though uncertainty is caused by the sheer number of soldiers transiting through on the 8/9 April 1917 – a fact which would have denied the opportunity to all but the most determined individuals. Of the two hundred and fifty names recorded on the walls so far analysed, few are dated between 8/9 April 1917.

During the war, the value of subways like Goodman was never questioned by those who fought, but in the years since, their contribution to the Allied victory on Vimy Ridge and elsewhere on the Western Front has often been overlooked. These modern conflict landscapes are multi-dimensional artefacts, and ambiguous palimpsests of time and space. 'Where does the mind stop and the rest of the world begin'?[29] If the Goodman Subway is understood solely by its physical structure then the relevance of humans to the creation of landscape is ignored. Therefore, attempting to understand how the soldiers in Goodman felt, how they experienced those hours and moments before the assault is a vital task. Broadly speaking, all the subways were similar in their construction[30] and the sensorial experiences and engagement of those that occupied them differed little.

Graffiti is often found together as those who left their mark sought to be part of the group. **(© Author/Durand Group)**

Goodman contains several carvings and this one is of particular interest. The face appears to be coming out of the chalk wall, a symbol of how men and landscape blended together in the subterranean world of modern warfare.
(© Author/Durand Group)

Names are usually written as opposed to carved, but this 3-dimensional example has been perfectly created and stands out from the tunnel wall.
(© Author/Durand Group)

However, there was no time to register these thoughts and feelings at the time, and those waiting to attack in the dark had more important things on their mind.

The better-documented Grange Subway counterbalances the limited available information on the human experience of the Goodman Subway during the battle. Since the late 1920's significant renovation has rendered a sizeable section of the Grange Subway publically accessible. Concrete has been added to stabilise the walls and roof, the floor has been levelled and surfaced with concrete, and artificial lighting has been added and props installed. These alterations ensure that the public are able to walk through, but the downside is that only the most basic appreciation of the soldier's engagement with this space is possible. Even so, as records exist of the conditions experienced in the Subway before the April attack, it's possible to combine them with the material culture, military realities, and the untouched physical remains of the Goodman tunnel to produce a more holistic appreciation of the events below ground immediately before the battle of Vimy Ridge.

The Grange, as with the Goodman, was constructed primarily as a communication subway and as a result had very little provision for the accommodation of troops. Despite this, on the evening of 7/8 April 1917 almost a thousand men moved into the tunnel to prepare for the attack. They were kept there for just under 36 hours[31], allowing them time to explore their sensorial relationship with this subterranean landscape, which was undoubtedly protecting their lives. Nevertheless, they endured appalling conditions. The sanitary situation was a sensual assault in its own right. With none allowed to leave, many would have had little choice but to defecate and urinate where they were, quickly turning the tunnel into a flowing latrine, polluting their clothes and equipment and filling the air with a gagging stench.[32] The proximity to human waste was a fact of life in the trenches[33], yet in this instance the effects were amplified due to the enclosed nature of the occupied space. The fear of what these soldiers were about to encounter further added to the misery, with many doubtless vomiting or sweating over what was to come, contributing to the noxious and anxious atmosphere. 'This is the trench. The bottom of it is carpeted with a viscous layer that clings noisily to the foot at every step and smells foul around each dugout

A section of the Grange is open to the public, offering a glimpse into the subterranean world of Vimy Ridge. However, metal, concrete, and artificial lighting all sanitise the space, much as with other subterranean sites open to the public on the Western Front. (© Author)

because of the night's urine. The holes themselves, if you lean over them as you pass, smell like a whiff of bad breath'.[34]

Soldiers were told to sit (on the now soiled floor) to allow air to circulate. With little or no ventilation along the entire length of the Subway the air quality was poor, leading to further discomfort and disorientation. The restricted and uncomfortable conditions of spending long periods in unnaturally cramped positions on uneven surfaces resulted in painful muscle aches and cramps, increased sensations of claustrophobia, and time for the mind to appreciate the severity of the situation. Despite the numerous bodies giving off heat, it was snowing on the surface and the ground was waterlogged, so liquid seeped through the walls of the tunnel, soaking those inside. The lighting was inadequate and men were not allowed to smoke due to the presence of explosives (although it is more than likely that some did, further adding to the polluted atmosphere). All this resulted in a miserable experience, and a completely alien sensorial engagement with the surroundings, 'officers were herded together in a grimy dugout, with bunk beds; the men were in long tunnels; and after a few hours of impervious sleep all woke to a sense of renewed misery'.[35]

Those in the subways were expected to wait in silence, unable to express either their fear or discomfort. The artillery bombardment of the German forward lines had begun on 20 March, intensifying on 2 April, and again on the eve of the battle. Total silence in subways was not always necessary, as they tended to extend from the rear to the front line trenches, but, in Goodman, the Subway had been dug out into No Man's Land, meaning that the German tunnels were by that point in very close proximity. It is not recorded whether the German pioneers were manning their listening positions prior to the attack, but those occupying the Subway would have been well aware that they could have been, reinforcing the relevance of noise, or its absence.

Outside, gas and high explosive shells screamed over No Man's Land, exploding amongst the German positions only a short distance away. The deafening noise mixed with the continual sound of machine guns harassing the German lines, created an unbearable cacophony, resonating off the walls of the Subway, causing vibrations that were felt by those waiting in the near darkness. As the walls and ceilings shuddered, the tunnels quickly filled with dust, choking still further the already rank atmosphere, and polluting what fresh water or rations there were. Gunner Frank Ferguson recalled the scene on the surface at the dawn of the attack as the bombardment reached its crescendo:

Was awakened this morning before daylight by a terrific bombardment. What a sight in the dim light as the guns put down the barrage for the boys to go over and try for Vimy Ridge. What a terrible racket as all the guns on the front blended into one continuous roar and the flashes from them made the effect of a great electrical storm.[36]

As dawn broke on the morning of the 9 April 1917 a wombat mine[37] was blown at the eastern end of the Goodman Subway. This formed a trench 51 m (170 ft) long by 10.5 m (35 ft) wide and 4 m (14 ft) deep that ran into the German front line. Two other exits were also opened in No Man's Land and saps were driven into the trench created by the wombat mine. To support the attackers making their way along the subways up to twelve trench mortar positions had been created. In Goodman, the men of the 8th Brigade of the 3rd Canadian Division, comprising the 1st, 2nd, 4th and 5th Canadian Mounted Rifles, were preparing to enter the annals of their young country's history.

At 5:30 am, after enduring the horrific conditions of the preceding hours, these men were sent forward. As the assault waves emerged, the mind had to cope with a different set of sensorial rules, as the claustrophobic subway gave way to the open trench, the experience of going over the top and then finally the chaos of the senses in a No Man's Land covered in April snow, and the unknown German trenches beyond.

The attack on Vimy Ridge by the Canadian and British XVII Corps was one of the greatest Allied successes of the war to that point, and the role played by the Goodman Subway during the battle cannot be underestimated. The Inspector of Mines report for an unnamed subway on the Ridge notes that 9,700 persons trafficked through it from 5 – 11 April – the equivalent of two complete fighting brigades in less than one week, an indication of the effectiveness of such tunnels.[38]

Subways were used on many First World War battlefields and were an effective way of protecting men from artillery barrages. The static nature of the Western Front meant that many subways were used over long periods of time, yet Goodman (along with the other subways on Vimy Ridge constructed for the April 1917 attacks) was built mainly for use on a single day, and therefore invites and offers a unique opportunity for an interdisciplinary investigation. All landscapes are palimpsests, geologically, culturally and symbolically constructed entities, and to more completely understand these complex artefacts, an approach is required that recognises the often-ambiguous relationship between people and the landscapes they create, and which in turn recreates those individuals. The sensual relationship between human beings and the places they inhabit does not just create space but also culture. By investigating these ambiguous landscapes from an anthropological perspective, it is possible to provide a more sensitised, nuanced and sophisticated context through which to understand the quotidian experiences of a soldier on the Western Front.

An invaluable part of the Durand Group's work in Goodman is the unpublished supplementary graffiti record, which details over two hundred and fifty examples, providing photos, location and relationships to other items. This raw data offers the opportunity for anthropological engagement via theories of agency, as well as providing a comparative data set for the investigation of other graffiti-bearing sites.

Future explorations of the Goodman Subway are dependent on several factors, of which arguably the most interesting are the politics of remembrance and of the continued deadliness of the landscape. Large parts of Vimy, including the area the Goodman occupies, are on land given to Canada in perpetuity after the war. It is considered sacred ground, not even open to the public, making it a highly contested area. It is also part of the Zone Rouge and the area needed to access the current entrance to Goodman is dangerous, and potentially lethal. Nevertheless, if access is granted in the future, it is clear that the Goodman Subway, and Vimy's other associated subterranean features, still have significant contributions to make to understanding the underground conflict of the First World War and all involved in it.

Chapter 6
The Verdun Inferno

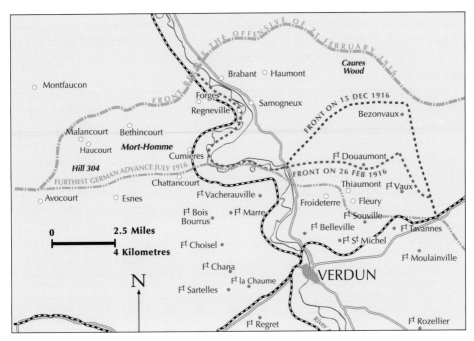

The Battle of Verdun lasted ten months and is the bloodiest battle in history. Fighting took place on both the left and right banks of the River Meuse. **(© Pen & Sword)**

An increasingly bloody phase of the war began in 1916. During the preceding months the opposing armies along the Western Front had reinforced their entrenched positions as they adjusted to the concept of industrialised warfare. Despite the appalling casualty figures of 1914 and 15, all knew that 1916 would be a decisive year. It was imperative that Germany regained the initiative after the collapse of her 1914 plans, and while the war in the east was producing some success, in the west things had stalled and Allied attacks were steadily wearing down the German army. On the Allied side, Britain and France's war economies had finally geared up to launch the grand offensives that would, they hoped, see the invaders expelled from France and Belgium.

The Allies had been planning a major assault on the Western Front since December 1915[1], and as the British Army recovered from the Battle of Loos and steadily grew in numbers again it had moved ever eastwards from Ypres and French Flanders, assuming a larger combat role in the conflict and thereby exerting more influence over events. By the first months of 1916, it was clear that a huge Allied force was planning to smash the German lines somewhere near the Somme River, and that this would almost certainly happen during the last weeks of summer. Before the British arrival, the Somme sector had been relatively quiet and the neat trenches with their frontage of precisely arranged barbed wire occupied by the Fourth Army showed little of the scars of war. Nevertheless, the daily German reconnaissance flights registered a change – a steady build up of stores behind the Allied lines, the influx of more British divisions and an increasingly aggressive posture in the opposite trenches told the Germans all they needed to know.

For the British, the Somme offensive is the defining event of 1916, if not the entire war. Yet the timing, conduct and outcome of those four months of ferocious fighting have their roots in another battle that took place some 300 km (185 miles) to the southeast, around the ancient French citadel of Verdun. It was here in February 1916 that the full industrialised might of this modern style of warfare was unleashed, making the confrontations of 1915 seem but a learning curve. Between February and December almost three-quarters of the French army would serve at Verdun, on a battlefield that came to hold the dubious honour for the highest density of dead per square yard in the history of warfare.[2] It would largely be an artillery duel, as both sides attempted to annihilate the other with the heaviest weaponry available, a consequence of which was that soldiers would be forced to seek the salvation of the earth more than ever before.[3]

Despite the prevalence of artillery, Verdun was perhaps also the most subterranean of all First World War battles. The citadel itself contained many underground catacombs and these were used for troop accommodation as well as to protect those civilians who didn't flee once the fighting began. In preparation for the onslaught, German assault troops waited in specially constructed stollen (man made concrete bunkers) as their guns hammered the French defences, which largely consisted of heavily defended forts and bunker complexes deep in the forests, hidden away beneath the dense dark tree canopy. Much of the fighting took place around and inside the concentric ring of subterranean forts that circled Verdun, and the overwhelming artillery presence ensured that trenches were demolished almost as soon as they were constructed, leaving soldiers to fight, often alone, for the possession of shell holes and mine craters, scars in the fabric of the tortured earth. Across most of the front living and fighting underground was a new and often overwhelming experience. At Verdun men's engagement with the landscape became more intense, more visceral and more immediate than almost anywhere else on the front lines. Soldiers didn't just utilise underground features, they became one with the earth. Living in squalor, surrounded by the dead who were constantly exposed and reburied by the violent shelling. The metaphysical boundaries between the body and the earth were not so much broken down as utterly destroyed. On the front lines, if there was such a thing at Verdun, everything was the earth; food, water, defences, weaponry, uniforms, life and death[4] – and it assaulted all the human senses.

Traces of these intense interactions can still be seen (and felt) today at the Trench of Bayonets, the imposing ossuary at Douaumont, the cratered battlefield of Thiaumont, at Vauquois, and in the lingering echoes of the eight destroyed villages that lie in the depths of the now replanted conifer forests. These new trees tower above the battlefield, their roots twisting through the many missing of Verdun and the millions of unexploded shells that still lie just beneath the surface, gruesomely entwining life, death, nature and the lethal legacy of modern warfare together deep beneath Verdun's countryside.

The descent

By the end of February 1916, neither the French nor Germans were strangers to a life underground. The Germans in particular had constructed comprehensive subterranean defences wherever possible and in preparation for the Verdun offensive, known as *Operation Gericht,* (or more literally *Operation Execution Place*) the German knowledge of subterranean defence was applied to the assault. During the preceding weeks they had constructed their deep stollen across the entire front, hidden in the forests immediately behind the planned attack zones. In places these huge concrete shelters were constructed to a depth of 15 m (45 ft). They could withstand heavy shelling and the largest would hold half a battalion of men.[5] The ability to accommodate so many soldiers hidden and safe was paramount to German general Erich Von Falkenhayn's plans, but it had a downside. To keep the stollen secret they had to be constructed far enough to the rear to avoid French reconnaissance aircraft, and this meant that in places the initial assault waves would have to cross 1000 yards of No Man's Land once the whistles blew. It was a calculated risk, and the absence of the usual jumping off trenches necessary for large scale attacks deceived the French. The Germans hoped too that the intensity of their pre-attack bombardment would destroy most of the deadly French 75 mm field guns, which, if left intact could seriously threaten their attack.[6]

As useful, and necessary, as the stollen were, they rapidly became hellish places. As dawn broke on 12 February those crammed inside readied themselves for the attack, but daylight revealed a grey wall of fog flecked with snow. Visibility was reduced to less than a 1000 yards, and the German gunners had nothing to aim at. In preparation for the attack they had amassed over 850 guns against a French total of 270, most of which did not have enough ammunition to repel the initial attack.[7] Yet, with zero visibility this massive artillery advantage was negated, so the battle was delayed. Those in the stollen, their nerves already on edge, remained underground for the next several days. In the fetid atmosphere conditions soon deteriorated – these subterranean sanctuaries had never been intended to accommodate men for long periods. There were only enough beds for a fraction of the troops and the terrible weather on the surface quickly flooded the bunkers. Men were forced to live underground knee deep in freezing water, which caused latrines to overflow, surrounding the attackers with their own filth and misery, blunting their effectiveness. The conditions soon took their toll and more and more of the elite storm troops began to complain of stomach troubles, either brought on by frayed nerves or the fetid environment.[8]

The two sides could not have approached the subterranean conflict more differently. To the Germans, the benefits of embracing the earth for protection were obvious. They had learned during the Allied attacks of the previous two years, and the stollen provided a logical progression from defence to attack. To the French, the idea of hiding below ground was anathema. The catastrophic defeat in the Franco-Prussian War of 1870/1 had largely been blamed on the absence of an aggressive fighting spirit or *élan*. By not taking the offensive the French never recovered from the two minor defeats of 1870, which rapidly led to further loss and retreat. Louis Napoleon's army desperately tried to hold off the far superior German force as it scrambled back towards Paris, but in the end it suffered the shame and bitterness of Sedan, only 65 km (40 miles) from Verdun. The same mistakes could not be made again and if the French wanted to rid themselves of the German invader then passively sitting beneath metres of earth was not the way to do it. As General De Castelnau proclaimed in 1913, 'the fortified places are a nuisance to me and they take away my men. I don't want anything to do with them.'[9] The French were aware that the Germans were constructing their stollen, but such was the Gallic distaste for defence, it was assumed that these underground bunkers were for protection from the French artillery, not to preserve the element of surprise for an attack.[10]

Despite the French reticence, there was an imposing collection of subterranean forts facing Crown Prince Wilhelm's army in February 1916. These formidable obstacles were a direct result of the 1871 defeat, which had left the new German border perilously close to Verdun. During the dying years of the nineteenth century it was clear to the French that the border along the Argonne had to be protected from the powerful new weaponry and enormous armies gathering in Germany. The answer was to add to and improve upon the existing fortifications, so that by the time the Battle of Verdun began, the Germans knew they faced twenty-eight mutually supporting modern forts, complete with all the advanced defences of twentieth century industrialised warfare. This defensive line appeared a formidable obstacle. Additionally, there were also ammunition depots, buried shelters and observation posts, all connected by narrow gauge railways and strategically sited roads.[11] The citadel's garrison numbered 66,000 men with enough supplies to hold out for at least six months.[12] It should have been impossible for the Germans to capture Verdun, or indeed to get anywhere near it.

Ironically, the Germans could not have been more wrong about the forts. By the time they had been built military thinking in France had moved on. As the dust settled on the 1871 defeat and France experienced a period of civil and martial unrest[13], the old, and now disgraced, school of military thought was banished, replaced with a new breed of officer that focused on the French fighting spirit. There would be no place for defensive ideology, for that train of thought led to Sedan. As Colonel de Grandmaison, the great French military thinker of the day, preached in warfare only two things are necessary, 'to know where the enemy is and to decide what to do. What the enemy intends to do is of no consequence.'[14]

Frontal assaults on entrenched positions were to prove fatal in the First World War, as de Grandmaison himself found out, killed before the end of 1914 trying to prove his point at the head of a doomed brigade.[15] It was too late for Verdun however, de Grandmaison's mad doctrine had infected the military psyche. The French army had to be fast, mobile and lethal. Anything detrimental to *L'attaque a outrance* was discarded – forts and heavy artillery were surplus to requirements.

The imposing forts that faced the German army through the Verdun mist in February 1916 were little more than an inconvenience to the French it seemed. The Germans didn't know that most of the heavy guns had been removed and replaced by fewer 75 mm field guns, devastating against enemy infantry but no match for the huge German Krupp artillery. Even though the first two years of the conflict had demonstrated how warfare now favoured the defender, the French dogmatic adherence to the spirit of élan meant they had been unable to change their philosophy by the beginning of 1916. The only protection from industrial weapons and massed assaults was the earth itself, and the relationship these modern soldiers had with it would be the deciding factor for France, both at the start of the battle and at its end.

While the French wasted time the Germans prepared to annihilate them. Their initial attack took place along a 12 km (7.5 mile) front stretching from the right bank of the River Meuse to the small village of Ornes, and on this narrow line the French would face more than 850 guns and 100,000 men.[16] Despite the privations of the stollen the storm troops they contained were relatively protected. The French, by comparison, were fully exposed to both the elements and the German artillery, which smashed the feeble trenches with alarming effectiveness. The waiting was almost over.

Hell on Earth

Before 1914 the village of Vauquois, sat peacefully atop a 290 m-tall hill on the edge of the Argonne Forest. It was home to some 170 inhabitants who lived in a small cluster of houses surrounding the village hall, a peaceful church and a bustling main street of shops situated on a plateau only 464 m (1332 ft) wide and 340 m (1115 ft) deep. It was the epitome of the French rural village, a place where the sounds of the church bells dictated life, forming a soundscape that many in turn of the century France would have understood.[17]

All this changed when war was declared. As the German armies swept into France the village was quickly occupied and by the end of 1914 the bells no longer determined daily life – their pleasing peals replaced by the harsh sounds of industrialised war. Vauquois' elevation made it a valuable and much-contested strategic location. In January 1915 the German 30th Pioneer Battalion had begun work underground, creating a new landscape that was to become the norm at Vauquois. As with much of the Western Front, from the terrible destruction emerged new creation[18] and soon after the German pioneers began digging beneath Vauquois the French followed suit, detonating their first mine charge on 17 February. It was the beginning of the most intense underground fighting on the Western Front, which would eventually lead to 519 mines being detonated beneath the Butte. By the middle of 1915 the fighting had become intense. The village was being transformed from a bucolic hamlet into a lunar landscape, and

519 mines were detonated beneath the Butte de Vauquois creating two hills from one, as the middle was blown away. There is nowhere else on the Western Front where this kind of intensely mined battlefield can be found. (© **Author**)

the intensity of the violence was magnified by the small space in which it took place. Soon trench lines were less than 10 m (30 ft) apart in places, and as the dead piled up on the surface life would increasingly be lived deep within the earth.

The scale of the destruction at Vauquois is difficult to quantify. Mine warfare intensified during 1915, and in the summer months alone the Germans blew fifty-one charges and the French seventy-seven.[19] Two out of three charges during 1915 broke the surface creating vast craters that consumed the remaining trenches and what was left of the village, but this was just the beginning of the apocalypse that would engulf the Butte. As well as mining, both sides were creating an underground world that could support thousands of men. The geology of the Butte consists of gaize, a type of sandstone perfectly suited to work underground. For the Germans, the work was made easier by the sheer drop from the Butte behind their lines. This enabled them to dig horizontally into the hill before digging down, offering protection from the French mortars and howitzers. As a result they were able to go deeper than the French, with tunnels as far down as 40m (130 ft), a depth that made them undetectable to the poilu in their listening galleries far above.[20]

A view of one of the French tunnels beneath Vauquois. Note the light railway tracks and extensive wooden supports. (© **Author**)

Throughout 1915 work gathered pace on both sides. The Germans built a narrow gauge railway to shift the spoil and both sides set up elaborate living quarters deep inside the hill. Hot and cold running water, electricity, ovens and communication equipment were installed, and both sides began to get used to subterranean life. On the surface almost nothing moved, except during trench

Both sides used light railways to transport the spoil from the underground workings. It was removed from the Butte and then disposed off as far away as possible in an attempt to hide the scale of the digging. (© **Author**)

raiding in the wake of mine detonations, as both sides sought to survive and prosecute the war. Life was becoming unbearable, but as the first shells crashed into the Bois de Caures announcing the start of the Battle of Verdun, life at Vauquois was about to become a living Hell.

Once the battle started the Butte assumed even more significance to both sides. The Islettes Pass, which the French reinforcements and supplies passed through on the way to Verdun, could be clearly observed from Vauquois. To the French the Pass contained the lifeline that would allow them to stem the German attacks. For the Germans it was a place that had to be shelled into oblivion. Only a week after the battle's initial attacks, on 3 March, the Germans detonated a 16,500 kg mine under the French positions on the Butte's eastern flank, at a depth of 35 m (114 ft). The result was devastating, and signalled the start of a tit-for-tat response as both sides tried to blow the other off the strategic hill.

The intensity of mine warfare above and below ground created a new world in which the human senses struggled to operate at all. Sight was restricted to the narrow view from trench periscopes, as snipers dispatched any who dared to look over the shattered parapets of trenches that were so close it was impossible to move around in daylight. Down below, the electric lighting failed continuously under the bombardments and relentless mining activity that cut cabling and

Today a monument stands on the site of the old Town Hall. The sculpted figures tell of the misery endured by both sides at Vauquois. (© **Author**)

shattered the piping carrying water and waste. The atmosphere in the dank tunnels deteriorated fast and the stench of human waste filled the subterranean passageways as faeces began to pile up, unable to be easily disposed of above. Jules Romains described the Butte as a 'refuse heap, house-wrecker's yard, cesspool and common sewer... A heap of ruins stuffed with dead men's bones.'[21] It was a place where the engagement of the senses defined space in the most visceral of ways.

> Paper soiled in no ambiguous fashion fluttered above narrow excavations at the bottom of which was heaped a browner filth, while here and there, between two stones set high on a trench wall oozed a trickle of black excrement... which the swollen flies found to their taste... let but the mind dwell on the thought of it, and the smell, here faint, there dense and obsessive, became a permanent feature of the place.[22]

With sight compromised, smell became a lifesaver as well as a tool for moving safely through the shattered landscape. Romain's hero, Clanricard, upon arrival at the Butte, lifts back a tarpaulin covering an entrance to the subterranean world, only to be physically shocked by the stench as he,

> Came to a full stop as though he had run his head against a wall. Impossible to find words strong enough to describe the atmosphere down there. It stood up like something solid through which he had got to force a way: 'thick enough to cut with a knife'. Every kind of foul vapour, everything least acceptable to nose and lungs, seemed to have been rolled and churned

together into a substance just not heavy enough to clutch with the hands, yet impossible to designate as air. There was something of every kind in it – bad breath, wind, the smell of wet dog, reminders of policeman's boots, of stale tobacco, even of the kind of fried-fish shop one comes across in the slums, and traces of suicide by charcoal fumes.[23]

The restrictive environment of the Butte amplified the fetid atmosphere. It was almost impossible for men to leave the safety of the tunnels to get fresh air without risking life and limb, so most simply stayed underground. Mining continued apace and on the 14 May 1916 the Germans detonated the largest mine of the war. It comprised a 60 tonne charge, delivered via the narrow gauge railway in five trucks, laid at the end of an 86 m (282 ft) long tunnel in a chamber 4.5 m (15 ft) wide and 2.7 m (8.5 ft) high.[24] The resulting blast created a crater 60 m (196 ft) in diameter, destroying 35 m (115 ft) of French line and demolishing the underground systems as far back as the third defensive line. 108 soldiers and 9 miners simply disappeared.[25] The explosion violently exposed the underground world to the surface, blowing men and material culture several metres into the air and then burying them again. The sheer scale of the blast added to the destruction

An aerial photograph of the Butte de Vauquois taken in 1918. The mine craters and extensive shell holes can clearly be seen. Although now overgrown, the Butte remains as it was during the war. (© **Public domain**)

of the battlefield, dissolving trenches, tunnels, No Man's Land, men and nature into a grotesque unidentifiable morass.

Conditions at Vauquois were so appalling that men on both sides struggled to comprehend such an alien world. Life above ground was impossible, and underground the Butte had become so riddled with tunnels that nowhere was safe. Nerves became frayed, every sound amplified, every sight exaggerated and every touch more tentative. Soldiers lived surrounded by the dead, in a place where the boundaries between life and death were corrupted. The cubist painter Fernand Léger noted on a visit to the Verdun sector,

> Human debris began to appear as soon as we left the zone where there was still a road. I saw excessively curious things. Almost mummified heads of men emerging from the mud. They were all small in this sea of earth. We thought they were children. The hands were the most extraordinary. There were hands I would have wanted to photograph exactly. That's what was the most expressive. Several had fingers in their mouths, fingers bitten off with teeth. I had already seen this on 12 July in the Argonne, a guy who was in so much pain he ate his own hands.[26]

The contortions imposed on the body by living underground in cramped spaces made men feel (or touch) in a very particular manner. No longer surrounded by air, soldiers were encased in damp gaize and continual contact with the earth made them more aware of their bodies. The darkness underground, and on the surface at night, emphasized the sense of touch, allowing life to be navigated more effectively. But touch played a different role, too. As Léger noted, dismembered bodies were a common sight and affected men in different ways.

> Oh the blood inside my body, fluid to the exquisite touch which, returning in its goodness, re-educates my body. My blood that I feel lick with the smoothness of velvet, first at the flesh in my core, then my appendages, the ravaged confines of my empire!
> I find you again, my stomach, and you, my individual fingers, which I name anew one after the other, commanding each to move. I return to my plenitude, and this second universe that is myself, hollow, as it must be so that I can be a man, fills again with life.'[27]

Men spent so much time worrying about death that eventually they became numb to it, 'all the same, you sleep and you eat near the charnel house, you even work there, and you keep smoking or laughing.[28]

The experience of Vauquois had a pronounced effect on André Pézard, who spent most of the 1916 battle there. He was a young scholar of Dante before the war and afterwards would go on to become France's foremost authority on the poet. Pézard undoubtedly saw much of Dante's Divine Comedy at Vauquois, as he too descended into the Inferno, 'The world was in its day of dark peril…'[29] The experience of the Butte was also not lost on Lawrence Binyon, a Red Cross orderly at Verdun and a future translator of The Divine Comedy.[30] The regularity of mine detonations at Vauquois reinforced the notion of a landscape of living Hell. The environment was in a constant state of flux, always shifting in the most literal manner, disturbing the buried dead and the location of the front line trenches (or what was left of them). André Pézard noted how the explosions created, 'a complete eradication, such an absolute transformation, as to seem at first too powerful to enter familiar eyes. I do not comprehend, I cannot.[31] The detonations themselves gave the impression that the earth was alive, and determined to consume those who wished to destroy it. To make matters worse, as so little could be seen the body had to process these seismic encounters primarily through touch and sound, which often overloaded the mind. When mine charges were detonated, the earth felt like it could give way entirely, plunging all on what remained of the plateau in to the depths:

> Suddenly he felt a shock. There could be no doubt of its significance. Ten seconds was enough for him to identify it. It seemed to strike from all sides at once at his sense of equilibrium. Had it come from the left or the right, from in front or from behind? Difficult to be sure. He felt as though he had been shaken to the roots of his being, as though there was no stable point left in the universe, as though he were a solid mass of liquid… It was followed almost at once by a deep, reverberating rumble that appeared to reach his senses through the medium of the shuddering earth around and ended, not by dwindling away into silence, but by a stifled roar, like as a thunder-clap deep in the bowels of the earth. Hard on its heels came other noises of creaks and crashes, of things falling to ruin that, in this hell of ruin, remained yet to be broken, of things thudding to the ground, hard things, soft things, things in a rain of atomised destruction; great solid lumps and tinkling fragments. He thought what he might have seen had he been better placed for seeing. But, for the moment, there was nothing for his eyes to note.[32]

These regular assaults on the soldier-body and its senses could not continue, although they went on long after the battle for Verdun was decided. By the end of 1917 life at Vauquois was abhorrent and men existed at the very limits of human endurance. Eventually, both sides agreed on an unofficial truce, only exploding mines in the morning so that there would be no casualties, with the Germans even apologising when on one occasion a mine was accidently set off at midday.[33] Then, at the end of December 1917, French and German miners came within a metre of each other deep inside the Butte. The French diggers heard German voices (speaking French) offering a truce[34] and both groups of diggers began to

At Vauquois parts of the battlefield restricted No Man's Land to only a few metres. (© **Author**)

Many of the gallery entrances are open at Vauquois, although those to the deeper systems remain padlocked. Tours of the tunnels can be arranged with Les Amis de Vauquois, the organisation responsible for the up keep of the site. (© **Author**)

sing their respective national anthems to each other.

Eventually the Germans broke the truce, but it was the beginning of the end of the Vauquois experience. Both sides had had enough. Lesser activity would take place there during the final year of the war as the Germans slowly retreated to the Hindenburg Line and the Allies pushed steadily forward. Vauquois fell to the US 35th Division on 26 September 1918 when they surrounded the hill and destroyed the remaining German defenders. The war had ripped the Butte de Vauquois in two. Beneath its shattered surface lay over 17 km (10 miles) of tunnels. The Germans had driven 12 km (7.5 miles) of this unique landscape of war, the deepest of which were more than 100 m (330 ft) beneath the surface. The French had managed over 5 km (3 miles). The village no longer existed, thousands had died and the (now) two hills were over 18 m (60 ft) lower than the single original had been in 1914.[35] Those who served at Vauquois had truly experienced the Inferno.

The Abyss

While Pézard and his fellow poilu were suffering at Vauquois, the main thrust of the Verdun battle was aimed at the forts that ringed the citadel. The Germans had utilised their stollen brilliantly, allowing for reinforcements to be quickly sent into the fray where they were needed most. The initial onslaught through the forests had, despite some delays, been largely successful. The great French General Driant had fallen, unable to stem the hordes emerging from the protective stollen, but his extreme courage was about to be wasted by the French ignorance of the importance of their own subterranean forts.

If the German attacks were to truly succeed then a major objective would be the capture of Fort Douaumont, and it appeared a seriously imposing obstacle. On paper, at least, Douaumont was the strongest fort in the world at the time.[36] It was constructed in the polygon shape so loved by the seventeenth-century French military engineer and fortification builder, Sébastien Le Prestre de Vauban. The fort measured more than a quarter of a mile across, and was protected by a sea of barbed wire 30 m (100 ft) deep, 2.5 m (8 ft) high spiked railings and a moat some

On paper Douaumont was impregnable. In reality it was nothing of the sort. Note the gun embrasures and machine gun ports, many of which had no guns in them during the initial stages of the battle. (© Author)

8 m (26 ft) deep.[37] Every approach was theoretically covered by either artillery, machine guns or cannon mounted in retractable cupolas, and searchlights continually swept the moat. Each defensive gallery was connected together via an underground passageway, which itself was defended with machine guns and moveable blockades, and the exterior of the fort was covered by its mutually supporting cousins, most notably the imposing Fort Vaux. Not only were the defences formidable, but also the fort's construction ensured that even the heaviest artillery the Germans could deploy would struggle to breach its walls. Only a fraction of the fort showed above the surface, a metaphor for most of the Western Front, but at Douaumont the subterranean world was encased in concrete, not chalk or wooden boarding. Beneath the surface was a maze of corridors, accommodation for a battalion of troops, subterranean escape tunnels, and enough water, food and ammunition to hold out almost indefinitely.[38] Fort Douaumont should have been impregnable. But it was not.

The French relationship with the new landscapes of war was nowhere near as sophisticated as their German equivalent. While the Germans were constructing their stollen, the French had been busy actually weakening their own subterranean defences. Most of the heavier guns had been removed during the previous years and used to support the infantry elsewhere on the front. Only a single 155 mm

A view through a defensive wall. When the French attempted to recapture the fort they faced the terrifying ordeal of fighting in narrow subterranean passageways often in complete darkness. (© **Author**)

cannon and two 75 mm field guns remained, encased in the retractable cupolas, and machine guns had replaced the other artillery pieces. Most criminally negligent of all, the garrison had been severely depleted, all in the spirit of élan. What stood in the way of the massed German forces was little more than a sheep in wolf's clothing.

As it was, Sergent Kunze of the 24th Brandenburgers single-handedly captured the 'mightiest fort in the world' on 25 February 1916. His unit had approached Douaumont on a routine reconnaissance patrol, and Kunze had noticed there was no defensive fire coming from the fort. He slipped down into the moat and up into the main structure through an open embrasure. Kunze was alone in the darkness, but already acclimatised after spending time in the stollen, he set off in search of the French defenders. First he came to a group manning the 155 mm gun. He arrested them and then came across another group of 20 attending a lecture by an NCO.[39] After locking up his captives Kunze then found the mess, and helped himself to a huge meal while the mayhem of the battle swirled away outside on the surface. His colleagues eventually joined him and the paltry number of French defenders was taken away. Douaumont was in German hands and it had fallen without a shot being fired. The cost to France of its recapture would be 100,000 men.[40]

Once again the Germans held the subterranean upper hand in the fight for Verdun. Fort Douaumont was a serious prize and its loss could have cost France the entire war. During the initial four days of fighting France had ignored the importance of the German stollen, and then the relevance of its own subterranean fortresses. Meanwhile, her soldiers were being massacred in open country by the vastly superior German artillery. Nevertheless, the French were still in possession of the other forts, and there was time during these early stages of the battle to reinforce them. But the High Command still didn't appreciate Germany's superior understanding of modern conflict landscapes, and if Douaumont was a catastrophe then Fort Vaux would be worse.

It took the Germans until June to be in a position to assault Fort Vaux, the smallest of the Verdun forts and only a quarter of the size of Douaumont. Even so, Vaux should have still been a serious obstacle. However, German shelling had knocked out the single 75 mm retractable turret and despite the three months that had passed since the fall of Douaumont, the remaining French 75s had been stripped from the fort and not replaced.[41] Fort Vaux stood naked and vulnerable, its only defence a few machine guns. Considering the fate of Douaumont this was inexcusable, but the defensive shortcomings were not the biggest problem. No escape tunnels had been dug, so the fort could not be relieved or resupplied. Despite repeated warnings, issues with the water supply had not been dealt with either. Additionally, extra men had been posted to the fort, so they were crammed in tight, leaving little room to manoeuvre. Originally designed to house 250 men,

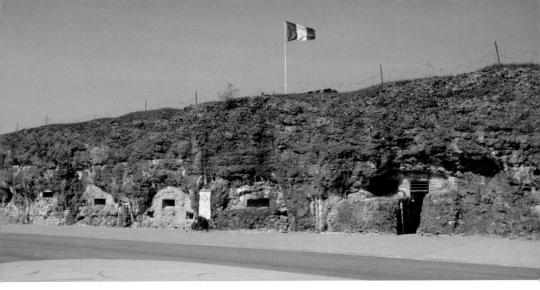

Although smaller than Douaumont, Fort Vaux was just as imposing. The French held on to Vaux for longer than Douaumont, but conditions inside quickly became inhuman. (© Author)

over 600 now sheltered inside the walls, many of them wounded. There were now more defenders than the fort's supplies could support.[42]

The Germans attacked on 1 June and although fighting was fierce it didn't take long for the assault waves to gain access to the fort, initially through a gap created by their artillery that had been hastily, and inadequately, blocked up with sandbags. By 4pm the Germans had taken the exterior defences and galleries, and were swarming about on the roof of the fort. When they got inside the fighting went underground.[43] For days the battle raged inside Vaux in narrow passageways bereft of light. The sound of machine guns echoed off the walls and the flashes from grenades lit the grizzly, blood filled corridors as both sides fought at close quarters. So narrow were the passages that it wasn't possible to

The French constructed brick and stone obstacles to protect their machine gunners. The attacking Germans had no such luxuries and were forced to use their own dead to protect the living. (© Author)

stand upright, making it impossible to take cover from the ricocheting bullets that tore into human flesh. The concussion from the grenades disorientated attacker and defender alike, and the fumes from the explosions, along with the stench of the dead, choked the lungs.[44]

The French fired their machine guns along the narrow corridors from behind concrete barricades and hastily improvised wooden defences. The Germans, having no such luxuries, were forced to create their own barricades from the bodies of their dead, firing through flesh at the embedded French. On 4 June the Germans brought up flamethrowers and attempted to burn out the French, but still they held on. In the end it was not bullets, grenades or fire that doomed the fort's defenders, it was water, or rather a lack of it.

So little attention had been paid to the fort's value that the water cistern had not been serviced. The gauge measuring the level in the cistern was defective and despite warnings as early as March nothing had been done.[45] Now Major Raynal, in charge of the fort's defence, had no water for the hundreds of remaining troops, many of who were now severely wounded. By the fourth day of the siege the Germans had taken possession of the last latrine, forcing the French to defecate and urinate where they stood. Disease began to break out and many came down with malaria. Dozens stood in the almost pitch black and freezing fort, riddled with fever as the walls shuddered under the weight of the German barrages. Soon, there was virtually no water left and what there was tasted of dead men.[46]

All efforts at relieving Vaux failed, feeding the desperation of those trapped inside. Through the still accessible upper parts of the fort, the desperate poilu could look through cracks in the superstructure and watch the men being sent to save them being annihilated. Many inside went mad, and one young lieutenant threatened to blow up the grenade store, preferring to die than try and live in the underground concrete prison any longer.[47] No one had had more than half a glass of water to drink for the past three days and men were now reduced to licking the moisture off the blood stained walls, or drinking their own urine, which made them wretch violently and increased their raging thirst.[48]. On the morning of the 7 June Raynal finally conceded defeat and surrendered the fort. As the survivors emerged from the depths their conquerors described them as the 'living image of desolation.'[49] and many crawled out of the fort on their bellies, like animals, and drank from the nearest corpse-filled shell hole.

Blood and filth and Verdun

The French did conduct subterranean operations across the Verdun front, but never as effectively as the Germans. On the left bank of the River Meuse both sides drove deep inside an aptly named hill, Le Mort Homme, and the French sappers dug extensive tunnels along most of the battle front, but again they were not properly used. The concept of using the ground creatively or even efficiently could not be balanced with the need to attack with Gallic flair. Even when subterranean spaces were used to good effect, a naivety was apparent, as was demonstrated on 4 September at the Tavannes railway tunnel. The tunnel was being used as a first aid post and temporary battlefield headquarters, but a fatal disregard of safety procedures for storing explosives led to a fire setting them off, causing the occupants to flee to the entrance, suffocated by the thick black smoke. No precautions had been taken to hide the command post and the German guns had zeroed in on the position. 500 men were blown to pieces at the gates of what should have been a subterranean sanctuary.[50]

The French paid dearly for their mistakes but as the battle unfolded a deeper and enduring connection was born, one that is still apparent at Verdun today. It was due to the way so many died and were then consumed by the mud and filth of the battle. At times man and landscape appeared indistinguishable. The flower of France's youth was being ground into the Motherland's soil, becoming one with it, uniting countryman and country together in the defence of the nation. Verdun had become sacred ground through the immeasurable suffering and deaths of its defenders.

Douaumont may have fallen without a shot being fired, but its recapture was amongst the bloodiest operations of the war. Before one attempt General Mangin declared to his men:

'The first wave will be killed.

The second also.

And the third.

A few men from the fourth will reach their objective.

The fifth wave will capture the position

Thank you, gentlemen.'[51]

The remorseless German artillery would destroy most of these soldiers. They were not just killed, but rather blown to pieces, often into microscopic fragments, which then became one with the earth. The attempts to capture Douaumont echoed similarly tragic efforts to relieve Fort Vaux. One stretcher bearer noted that the closer the attempted relief got to Vaux the worse the debris of battle became, and almost every shell hole contained at least one corpse:

Some on their back, others on their stomach. Some, mown down in a bayonet charge, still clutch their rifle butts. Others have been felled at their machine gun posts. Human remains everywhere, mangled limbs. Sticking out of the half flattened trench we are following, here, there, an arm, a leg, a head.[52]

The situation was so bad that relief parties approaching the fort reported that they were digging trenches not through soil but through '*viande*' (meat).[53] By the latter stages of the battle this human/meat metaphor had become reality, as soldiers bleated like sheep while making their way from Verdun's precious artery, the *Voie Sacrée,* to the front line.[54]

This level of carnage is difficult to imagine, and even the raw statistics struggle to comprehend it. By June, only four months into the battle, it is estimated that over 24 million shells had been fired into the constricted Verdun sector, and by the end of the battle over 1,000 shells had been expended for each square metre of the battlefield.[55] This 'munitions landscape' was a mix of man, materiel and mud, yet in such a terrifying place, despite the terrible cost, France prevailed, forever forging a link between the sacred soil of Verdun and those who gave their lives for the glory of France.

Nowhere on the Verdun battlefield is this connection better displayed than at the *Tranchée des Baionettes* (Trench of Bayonets), a place of legend that lies in the Ravine de la Dame, shadowed by the heights of Thiaumont, and the imposing Douaumont ossuary. On 10 June 1916, the 3rd Company of the 137th Regiment was manning a badly-positioned trench which was being mercilessly raked by German artillery. The 137th were from the Vendée region of the country, which

La Voie Sacrée was the name given to the only serviceable road into Verdun. The French Army had to ferry all the men and supplies required for the battle along its length, and keeping the traffic flowing was of prime importance. (© Author)

Much of the battlefield is left as it was, a scar on the heart of France. (© **Author**)

had a reputation for supplying France with some of her toughest fighters.[56] Yet toughness alone offered little protection against the overwhelming German artillery. At roll call on the evening of the 11 June only 70 men remained from an initial figure of 164, and by the following morning the 3rd Company of the 137th no longer existed, their colonel saying that only a Second Lieutenant

The last resting place of the brave men of the Vendée is memorialised at Verdun inside a concrete sarcophagus. (© **Author**)

and one man remained.[57] The rest were nowhere to be found, declared to have been lost to heavy shelling while stoically manning their posts. Quickly this gallant defence became the stuff of legend and in December 1917 a French Army commission was ordered to Verdun to confirm the incident. The commission spoke to a French pilot who had flown over the area on 12 June 1916 and had reported seeing the ground move, as if by an earthquake.[58] The story perfectly encapsulated the French efforts at Verdun. These brave soldiers had given their lives defending the sacred heart of France, but more importantly, they had been consumed by the very soil they sought to defend, swallowed whole by the earth, taken into the bosom of the Motherland, and become one with France.

The exact fate of 3rd Company was not discovered until after the war, when in 1919 the commander of the 137th visited the battlefield and discovered numerous rifles protruding from the earth in 3rd Company's last known location.[59] When the area was excavated a body was found under each rifle, still manning the trench, and still defending France. It was decided that the 3rd had probably placed their rifles on the parapet in preparation to fend another German assault and had then been buried alive during the ensuing attack.[60] In this way, the myth was born.

More than likely, the 3rd were destroyed by artillery or the advancing Germans, who then filled in the trench as they passed by, perhaps leaving the rifles exposed as a mark of respect.[61] It didn't really matter – the exact cause of their death was no match for the myth and legend. The French Army commission of 1917 had already decreed that the trench should be preserved, and when the American banker, George F. Rand visited the area at the end of 1919 he was so moved by

Crosses now stand in for the bayonets, which have long since been stolen by trophy hunters. (© **Author**)

the destruction he saw that he offered the French government 500,000 Francs to memorialise the last stand of the 137th.

An austere concrete memorial was constructed over the 'trench' and the bayonets and rifle tops were replaced and cemented into the ground (the originals had long since been stolen by battlefield tourists), but so horrifically destroyed and devastated had the area been that it was almost impossible to be sure of the exact location of the 137th's last stand. Likely, it was around 30 m (100 ft) away from the memorialised version on a shell-cratered stretch of land, but on a battlefield that consumed so many men, this didn't seem overly important. Even so, it meant that this memorial designed to reinforce the legend of France's finest hour was itself a 'site of myth'.[62]

The Trench of Bayonets perfectly announces the way that men and the earth were made one at Verdun. Soldiers prepared for attack in the ground, fought in the mud, occupied the forts built deep into the earth, and they died in the morass. And it was not just earth, it was the symbolic body of a country, devouring the enemy and folding its brave warriors in an eternal embrace. This notion of the soil of France protecting its soldiers and helping to defeat the German invaders needed to be memorialised, and the intensity of the destruction at Verdun provided the perfect candidates. The nine villages ground to pieces during the battle.[63] Beaumont, Bezonvaux, Cumières, Douaumont, Fleury, Haumont, Louvemont, Ornes, and Vaux no longer existed after 1916. They had been pulverised into nothingness and then blown by the wind to the four corners of France.

The village of Fleury was completely destroyed during the battle. Today the streets have been marked out and the main businesses represented by small stones. It is a ghost of its former self, but its sacrifice will never be forgotten in France.
(© Author)

Of the nine destroyed villages, Fleury-devant-Douaumont is probably the best known. Before the war Fleury had a population of some 500 people, all of who left before or during the early stages of the battle. By the end of the summer there was virtually no trace of it, save for a white smear visible from the air and a silver chalice found on the site of the former church.[64] Once the fighting ceased it was possible to walk over the site without even knowing the village had ever been there – it had become, 'Nothing; The whole place has returned into dust, with the bones of the thousands of adversaries who rushed here pell-mell it had become a chaos of shadows in this village of shadows.'[65] Today Fleury has been 'recreated' in ghostly form. The village streets appear as paths twisting through the replanted forest, white stones with plaques dotted along their length mark the locations of former shops, the village school and other civic sites. The only building that stands is a small chapel of remembrance and reconciliation, and similar ones are found at the other eight villages. All nine still retain their legal status and mass is said in the chapels once a year. They even have an elected mayor.

Verdun's martyr villages and the Trench of Bayonets perfectly encapsulate how at Verdun Frenchman and France became one. At Verdun combatants fought from shell hole to shell hole in a landscape dismembered by explosives where there were no trenches and it was impossible to tell French from German, all were the colour of earth.'[66] On the 7 August 1932, adjacent to the blood-soaked stretch of battlefield known as the Ouvrage de Thiaumont and above the Ravine de la Dame, the tragically imposing Douaumont ossuary and cemetery was officially opened.[67]

The first stone was laid in 1920 and the construction was largely paid for by donations, many of which were garnered by the Monsignor Ginisty who was Bishop of Verdun from 1916-1945.[68] After the war, as the remains of soldiers were retrieved from the battlefield, enormous bone mountains began to appear at Verdun. These macabre heaps of human ruin needed a final resting place and the ossuary today contains the remains of some 130,000 men, the bones of which can be seen through windows along the length of the building, lest anyone forget the price France paid to hold Verdun. The ossuary itself is almost a quarter of a mile long and appears as a sword slammed into the ground up to its hilt, again reinforcing the connections between the landscape and those who fought and died. Some say its tower also represents an artillery shell.[69] Inside are forty-six stone coffins, each representing a different sector of the battlefield, and each containing further human remains from the area. There is also a small museum and chapel along with images of some poilu that survived, pictures of them during 1916 alongside others depicting them in old age, showing that despite the carnage some did survive. The cemetery in front of the ossuary contains 15,000 graves, reminding the visitor that many did not.

The cemeteries outside the ossuary are the final resting place of over 15,000 French soldiers from the Motherland and the colonies. Inside are the unidentified remains of more than 130,000 soldiers, both French and German. (© Author)

The legacy of Hell

By 1916 the Germans had become experts in subterranean warfare. At Verdun their construction of numerous stollen demonstrated this creative military engagement with the earth. The German embrace of underground warfare was not without risk and many men still lie entombed in long-forgotten stollen, as they do in the casemates that pockmark the battlefield. With much of the area still off limits to the public due to the vast quantities of unexploded munitions, it is unlikely that their bodies will ever be recovered. In one casemate near Fort Douaumont a German medical officer, Stefan Westmann, recalled seeing a sign pinned to the bricked-up entrance. It read, 'Here lie 1,052 German soldiers', a whole battalion of men had been killed when the fuel used by the flamethrowers had exploded. Such was the carnage that these men were simply bricked up into their readymade grave and left in peace.[70]

The French had not learned the lessons that had so benefited the Germans, and they paid for this folly with the blood of thousands. France recorded some 378,777 casualties during the ten month battle (the German figure was 330,000).[71] For France it was after the battle the realisation dawned. The neglect displayed towards the forts would not be repeated – France could ill-afford to expend the lives required to retake Fort Douaumont again, and this led directly to the construction of the Maginot line.

This vast stretch of defences, consisting of trenches, forts, barbed wire, tank traps, machine gun and artillery positions was intended to protect France's borders from further aggression. It was completed in 1940 and named after the former French Minister of War, André Maginot, who had a been a major advocate of the project. It was indeed a formidable obstacle. The scars of Verdun ran deep and when the Germans invaded France again in May 1940, the poilu sought the safety of the earth over the dashing infantry charges of élan.

To the Germans it was obvious how effective subterranean defences could be against the static lines of the Western Front, but conflict had evolved since by 1940. The Germans had graduated to a new style of warfare, one that relied on speed and movement, not forts and entrenched positions that bogged down attacks. Rather than attempt to breach the Maginot Line the Germans simply went around it, driving their Panzer Divisions through the thick forests of the Ardennes, an area the French considered to be a natural defensive line, impassable to tanks. Again, the French were behind the times, and the Germans ruthlessly exploited their ignorance.

After 1918 every city, town and village in France was given an urn of Verdun's sacred soil to be positioned for all to see before local war memorials. Almost three quarters of the French army had served at Verdun, and the experience of that battle was not allowed to die. Its legend steadily grew and stories of the valiant stand against the old enemy were passed down to new generations, almost all of which had a father or grandfather who had served in the maelstrom of Verdun. Today the citadel still feels oppressed by the weight of history. Much of the battlefield still bears the wounds; the trees are all young, the bunkers and forts still exist, the whole area hides the lethal legacy of industrialised warfare, and the bones of unidentified French soldiers from across the Western Front are interred in the ossuary at Douaumont. Most important of all, Verdun proves that out of the most visceral and intense destruction this new warfare created new relationships between man and the earth – on a scale unlike anything seen before in the history of conflict.

The inside of the ossuary is a hallowed place. Large photos of soldiers during the battle and in old age are a reminder that despite the terrible losses France did prevail. Verdun did not fall. (© **Author**)

Chapter 7
Digging in the Dark

Military History has overshadowed the study of the First World War for almost a century, unconsciously shaping the way that archaeologists, anthropologists and the general public have approached the conflict and its legacies. Yet if we seek the human experience of the conflict, it will not be found in trench maps or unit designations, types of weaponry or casualty figures. It will be found on and beneath the landscape and in the relationship that soldiers and civilians had with it.

By the end of 1914, it was clear that the nineteenth century concept of a battlefield could no longer be applied to landscapes where modern methods of waging war were involved. Hitherto unimaginably powerful weaponry, produced on an industrial scale, ensured that armies could no longer offer battle in the grandiose manner of Napoleon or Wellington's forces.

At the Battle of Mons in August 1914, the Germans advanced on the British positions across the Mons-Condé canal in traditional columns. A century before the width of the canal would have ensured that both sides were at the limit of their effective musketry range, but that day in August, as hundreds of men approached

The Germans advanced on the British across the Mons-Condé canal in column. They were cut to pieces by witheringly accurate rifle fire. (© **Author**)

the banks in the manner of Napoleon Bonaparte's Old Guard, they walked out of the past and into the future of warfare.

Trained soldiers could now fire fifteen aimed rounds a minute from powerful and accurate modern rifles.[1] The German mass attacks at Mons were simply 'shot flat', creating piles of corpses in seconds.[2] It was clear from the start that combat had changed dramatically. So devastating was the British rate of fire, that the advancing Brandenburg Grenadiers were convinced they faced multiple machine guns, whereas in fact the 1st Battalion Queen's Own Royal West Kent Regiment possessed only two of these weapons.[3] British rifle fire was supported by heavy artillery, which, over the next four years, would turn battlefields into multi-dimensional battle-zones where the living and the dead intimately shared the same ground for years. Industrial quantities of dead and wounded would be produced by the sheer quantity of high explosive delivered by endless artillery bombardments, and by shrapnel weapons, machine-guns, grenades, gas and aerial bombing. Much of the ordnance expended remains live, and this enduring legacy of volatile unexploded munitions is a defining characteristic of modern conflict landscapes, totally absent from all battlefields that preceded them.

The consequences of adapting to life in these new conflict landscapes often resulted in severe mental and physical trauma. Shell shock was diagnosed for the first time, and men had to cope with the mental challenges of surviving in a lethal and constricted space. Life inside the earth required a complete renegotiation of body and environment. Gas masks restricted vision and movement across the battlefield, hearing was dulled and new haptic elements of warfare were

Designed by W.S Allward and unveiled by King Edward VIII on 26 July 1936, the imposing Vimy Memorial is dedicated to all those Canadians that served in the First World War. It bears the names of the 11,161 Canadian soldiers who died during the conflict and have no known grave. (© **Author**)

Designed by Sir Edwin Lutyens and unveiled on 1 August 1932, the Memorial to the Missing of the Somme at Thiepval, bears the names of 72,246 officers and men of the United Kingdom and South African forces who died in the Somme sector before 20 March 1918 and have no known grave. Those never found from other parts of the Commonwealth have their names displayed on other memorials in the area.
(© **Author**)

Situated on Ypres' eastern walls, the Menin gate was designed by Sir Reginald Blomfield and unveiled on 24 July 1927. It displays the names of 54,398 officers and men who lost their lives in the Ypres Salient and have no known grave. The names of many more with no known graves appear on other memorials in the area.
(© **Author**)

experienced. High explosive reduced men to nothing more than pink mist, and war was waged in three dimensions, above, on and below the surface. The resulting new landscapes of industrialised war destroyed all previous concepts of the soldier's sensorium while simultaneously creating new ones.

Once the war ended the battle-zones changed again as the conflict was commemorated and those that died were memorialised. Permanent cemeteries were built on land given in perpetuity to the belligerent nations. Grand monuments were created and the war was represented according to national preference. Remembrance on this scale was unheard of before the onset of industrialised war, and it further changed the fabric of the landscape, making it clear that modern conflict landscapes would have what can be called a 'continuing biography of conflict'. The spaces of warfare were reconfigured, as was the soldiers' corporeal engagement with them; continuously broken down, rebuilt and recycled. The majority of personal accounts from the war[4] and some scholarly works[5] allude directly or indirectly to this metamorphosis of mind and matter.

The post-1918 social life of the Western Front has ensured that much of the front line landscapes described in this literature have disappeared from view, hidden beneath many recent layers of memory, memorialisation, tourism and commemoration. Yet, the subterranean conflict landscapes explored in this book, and the diverse material culture they contain, still exist beneath the dynamic Western Front. They are not easily identified or accessed, and are often misrepresented as a sideshow or secret war, when in reality they were an integral part of trench warfare. The human experience of living and fighting in an industrial war can be understood primarily in terms of the sensual engagement between man and landscape – the Western Front was just as much a sensescape as a landscape.

The underground war was dark, and sight gave way to the other senses as a result. Sound replaced vision, often felt through the vibrations of exploding ordnance, producing a new element to the power of touch. Haptic engagement was essential, but rather than one sense becoming dominant, the application of the entire range of the senses changed. Individuals can change and adapt the ways their bodies engage with the world at will, although not always without behavioural consequences, something shown by the war experience of so many soldiers who journeyed from being civilians to soldiers and back again.

Darkness ruled on the front line, and work was carried out at night. The days were spent out of sight in trenches, travelling along subways, labouring underground with tunnelling companies, sleeping in funk holes and dugouts, or waiting to go into battle in souterraines and deep dugouts. The cultural capital of vision[6] so prized in Westernised countries had little value in this modern world of war.[7]

The daily life of soldiers and tunnellers divided the senses. Unless waiting below ground to go into battle or working with tunnellers, infantry soldiers in the front line usually experienced darkness only at night. For the tunnellers and others underground, darkness was omnipresent and daylight restricted. The deprivation of the senses was as commonplace as their reconfiguration. Those underground experienced this deprivation on a daily basis, an experience only shared by those on the surface when they left the trenches during attacks, often wearing gas masks while charging through the smoke, fumes and mud.

Tunnellers frequently had to fight hand to hand in the dark and restricted underworld. Despite their best efforts to remain silent, the listening devices used by both sides often caught the enemy unaware. The silence of monotonous digging could be interrupted at anytime, replaced with the aural chaos of an underground breakthrough. Men on night-time trench raids underwent a similar experience. As they crawled silently towards the enemy lines barbed wire had to be quietly cut, coughs and the sound of breathing suppressed, movement controlled. As they slipped into the enemy trench with club in hand[8], the body and mind had to adapt to the chaos of sudden combat in a dark, strange and restricted space.

So severe was this new human engagement with the immediate world that comparisons with contemporary Western cultures and societies are often inadequate, making it necessary to look further into the past, and also to study the lives of non-Western cultures whose engagement with the environment differs from our own.

Global war involves an eclectic mix of cultures and nations, yet in 1914 none could have fully appreciated the confusion that the human body would experience on the Western Front. So intense were these physical and psychological experiences that they created a 'No Man's Land of the senses' where often the only common denominator shared by those present was their humanity. National, cultural and individual attitudes to life, society, religion, taboo, ritual, politics and bodily engagement with the world were shattered and remade as hundreds of thousands of individuals were drawn into a 10,000 km^2 (6,213 mile^2) area of Northern Europe.

Throughout history there has always been a cultural dimension to the front lines of war. To stand in a shield wall, face a cavalry charge or exit a landing craft onto a corpse-strewn beach, soldiers developed a shared approach to war-life. The deprivations of POW and Internment camp life were the same, as wars could often find men (and women) living in challenging circumstances, separated from homes and families for long periods. In all modern conflict (and in different ways in pre-modern conflicts, too) human senses have played a critical (if often under-acknowledged) role in understanding these shared experiences. The chaos of an American artillery bombardment in the jungles of Vietnam[9] during the 1960s was as much a sensorial endeavour as the Trojans resisting the relentless attacks of the Greeks during the siege of Troy.[10]

Surviving subterranean conflict on the Western Front similarly demanded a shared understanding of war-life, which led to an inversion of normal everyday behaviour, which led to what might be called a hybrid subterranean conflict culture. It developed because the First World War created a radically different kind of battle-zone to any conflict that preceded it, and, arguably, to any that have followed since. The inertia of the Western Front, a landscape repeatedly saturated with high explosive, iron and steel meant that life and death coexisted in exactly the same space for days, weeks, months and sometimes years, and the human reaction to this drastically altered the way that the senses engaged with this new reality. Fighting in and under the ground was not new in 1914, and neither was an affinity between combatant and the battlefield, but the Western Front's amplification of this relationship was so intense that it left deep scars on the lives of those who experienced it.

The language used to describe these unnatural and disturbing war experiences is often zoomorphic; humans 'slithered', 'crawled' and 'burrowed'.[11] Landscape was considered in anthropomorphic terms, too; 'watching', 'consuming' and 'slobbering'.[12] Some authors have mistaken this language to mean that because soldiers spoke such words, they believed themselves somehow transformed into animals, living in the earth and losing their grip on the essence of what it means to be human. This narrative fits with the history of the conflict provided by revisionists[13]; that people were slaughtered like animals, and saw their enemy (and sometimes themselves) as little better than vermin. Alan Clark's (1991) best-selling book *The Donkeys* played on such imagery, influencing attitudes to the conflict for decades.

That soldiers on the Western Front lived in and beneath the ground in primeval conditions is undeniable. So too is the fact that the war changed the relationship between landscape and people. Images of soldiers up to their waists in mud, filth and water testify to these 'truths' and the narration of the war through photography, film and innumerable texts further amplifies these impressions, elevating them from one aspect of front line existence to the apparent reality of everyday life.

Soldiers during the First World War created a subterranean world of 'artefacts and monuments', enduring inhuman conditions yet crafting a very human landscape. The evidence is incontrovertible, embedded in works of art, carved, scrawled and built out of and into the geology of the battle-zones. It is apparent in the use of building materials and the more aesthetic decorating of the subterranean landscape with pictures and furniture. The hospitals, living accommodation and places of worship constructed deep below ground in the chalk of Picardy, Artois and elsewhere contributed to a cultural environment where human values were preserved, gods were worshipped and the dead were buried – all distinctly human behaviour in the chaos of war.

The complexity, scale and engineering prowess of the subterranean landscape shows the time, manpower and expenditure lavished on keeping soldiers as safe as possible, recognising that the preservation of their humanity was essential if they were to be effective combatants. The material culture this landscape still contains proves how men clung to their identity beneath the surface. All the senses actively engage with the environment, and via this reciprocal process soldiers embraced their animal instincts to survive.

The case studies presented in this book show how modern interdisciplinary investigations of First World War subterranean landscapes have developed over the last fifteen years, and how they are integral to understanding the battles that raged on the surface. The battles described here have deliberately allowed for the underground aspects of each event to be placed within the wider narrative. Loos, Vimy and Verdun are all engagements that have been endlessly analysed and published.[14] Significantly, the subterranean dimensions of conflict at Vimy and Loos described here rely heavily on the work of the Durand Group, and thus are able to incorporate archaeological and anthropological information and insights. Verdun was different, relying less on the Durand Group and more on my own fieldwork conducted over the past five years. The Copse tunnel system at Loos-en-Gohelle is amongst the most dynamic and ambiguous subterranean spaces I have personally experienced, and much of it had not been explored since the Second World War, so it is a conflict-related time capsule in its own right. The dimensions of Copse, the types of military features it contained, its multi-level structure and its geographical links to the wider subterranean landscape are all of prime archaeological and anthropological importance. However, it was the experience of spending long periods in the system that revealed its qualities as a sensescape. Crawling through fluctuating water levels, working at various depths, feeling changes in airflow and air quality, and a haptic engagement with the chalk tunnel boundaries all allowed for a comparison with the soldier's experience, reinforcing the notion that 'human beings live in, and not on, the world they create'.[15]

The Copse system was initially used to listen for the approaching enemy, and to help destroy German offensive and defensive underground efforts. For much of the war Copse was part of the British front line positions, a lethal and highly ambiguous place, and modern research fieldwork is clearly not capable of replicating these conditions; but as the conflict progressed the system's war-life demanded a change of use, eventually removing Copse from immediate threat as the lines moved forward. Once this danger had passed the tunnel system's characteristics changed, and the experience of being in the system is very much the same today as it was in late 1917 and 1918.

The inherent dangers of being underground are still present; the atmosphere is similar, as is the sensorial interaction with the space, increasing the archaeological relevance of a phenomenological engagement with it. The ability to control the senses in an alien landscape was something I experienced during my research. Archaeological and anthropological investigation of First World

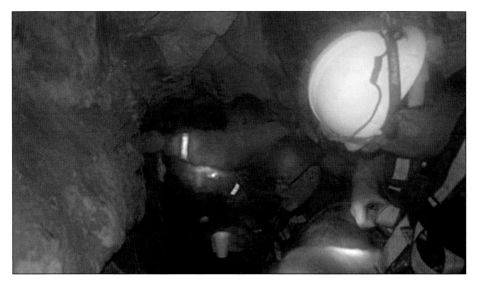

Members of the Durand Group taking a well-earned break during fieldwork in the Copse tunnel system **(October 2012)***. Space was limited, lighting poor, and the environmental conditions oppressive. (© Author/Durand Group)*

War subterranean landscapes is not possible alone, yet in these confined and hazardous places, the bodily control required to operate effectively is noticeable, and is often experienced simultaneously as a team. Tunnel walls are constantly felt for reassurance, or to anchor the body in place, even in the illumination of modern LED lighting. The way the ground feels is communicated more precisely as the feet independently search for a sure footing in the slippery gloom, defining space through the feet as well as the hands.[16] A fine powder of chalk continually affects one's sense of taste. Sound travels in peculiar ways along passageways, affected by the mediums it passes through, showing that different places sound different, and often the constant noise and flashing lights of air monitors and gas alarms further confuses the soundscape.

In such hazardous places, my Durand Group colleagues and I are often in close proximity, something absent from the majority of 'civilian' work-life where personal space (and all that this means for our society) can be respected. Underground it is different. Crawling through dark and constricted passageways, individuals stay close together, often relying on each other for assistance. There is regularly a lack of oxygen, constant danger of collapse and difficulties experienced navigating through a complex, constricted and multi-levelled space. The implementation of modern archaeological and anthropological procedures therefore provided a revised appreciation of the soldier's experience. When these findings are combined with a military understanding of the battles fought on the surface, personal accounts, memoirs and diaries of those serving in the Loos sector, a more nuanced and insightful appreciation of life in this particular part of the Western Front is possible, as is a more sophisticated understanding of how subterranean warfare developed during the conflict.

Just as the interdisciplinary investigation at Copse revealed much about the consequences of the Battle of Loos, the Durand Group's work at Vimy demonstrated how the lessons learned at Loos were there in 1917. The dimensions of the Goodman Subway, its purpose, the exposure of the material culture contained within, the Subway's place in the wider battle-zone, as well as how these features affected the prosecution of battles were all original and important discoveries. In the years that followed these initial surveys, a more complete assessment has emerged that appraises the Subway as an artefact, appreciating its continued 'social life' as part of a dynamic palimpsest landscape. An anthropological investigation of the Subway's material culture and a knowledge of the human corporeal engagement with it have all greatly contributed to the understanding of the existential experience of being in this type of subterranean location.

By 1917 soldiers had become more adept at spending time underground, more aware of the benefits of using subterranean features such as subways, and consequently they were better prepared to face the demands of the front, allowing mainly conscripted soldiers to become professional warriors. The subways had become more commonplace right across the front as this realisation increased,

Space in fighting tunnels is extremely limited, forcing the body to endure discomfort for long periods. (© **Author/Durand Group**)

producing a symbiotic relationship between contemporary soldiers and the subterranean landscape of the front.

Likewise, the Durand Group's work at Maison Blanche has revealed it to be far more than just a subterranean void used (primarily) by First World War Canadian soldiers. As this former quarry experienced a social and cultural interaction with soldiers, its biography developed, creating a new form and purpose. By spending time in the souterraine the soldiers that occupied it adapted themselves to the demands of a modern and industrial war and an ontological study of the souterraine hinted at the mindset of those who experienced it before, during and after the conflict. Wartime carvings and graffiti on the walls showed the corporeal human truths of being in these places during times of war and should be regarded as the monikers and markers of an inverted cultural experience.[17]

Through fieldwork the constant temperature and the effect illumination had on the perception of space and place could be studied. Thus the sensorial experience of Maison Blanche could be added to the existing data regarding its location and role in the war, creating a more sophisticated and sensitised understanding of this place in particular, but also of similar locations along the Western Front. Its relevance extends also well beyond the First World War, to many analogous twentieth and twenty-first century subterranean conflict landscapes.

The first two case studies show how underground landscapes were an intrinsic element of the Western Front, and how these features were employed depending on the military demands of each sector at different stages of the conflict. They also introduce the connections between human beings and nature in modern warfare, showing how individuals and groups can control their engagement with even the most hostile of surroundings. These understandings allow for a battle as complex as Verdun to be approached and reappraised from a more humanistic point of view, exposing the horrific destruction mechanised warfare caused to landscape and the human body. At Verdun the boundaries between nature and humanity became almost meaningless as the landscapes of above and below were blasted together. Men lived not on or in the earth but with it, elevating the concept of subterranean warfare out of the depths.

Throughout this book I have endeavoured to show how underground proximity to the firing line, military purpose, and size of features varied as subterranean systems were recycled and reconfigured as the war developed. Tunnellers, used to being underground, created or adapted the subterranean systems, but engineers and infantry would not have been so comfortable in these places. As a result, those sharing these spaces would not necessarily have experienced the same sensorial sensations, just as individuals do not have identical experiences of landscape. This reinforces the ambiguity of modern conflict landscapes, and particularly of subterranean ones, which are confused palimpsests within palimpsests, and consequently are often difficult to define and understand. Any subterranean system could change its status almost instantaneously if the lines moved forward, attacks were successful, enemy positions were captured, defensive locations were required in No Man's Land, or tunnels were blown by enemy sappers. This dynamic demonstrates the ability of the human senses to add to our understanding of war experience.

There are other areas of First World War research where an anthropology and archaeology of the senses could prove useful. Traditional approaches to the archaeology of the conflict suffer because the complex relationships between its landscapes and objects are misunderstood, or elided in favour of rare or more tangible artefacts. Yet not all artefacts can be touched or even seen. The constantly changing relationship between soldiers and landscapes, and the way that the senses contribute to the experience of life are harder 'artefacts' to identify, but they are just as relevant. Approaches to culture, religion, food, clothing and taboo are all objectified in the material culture of the Great War. Recognition of the dynamic and ambiguous nature of modern conflict can offer a powerful assessment of the landscapes and objects of war, as well as those who lived and died within them.

The way that warfare is corporeally engaged with changed forever in the battle-zones of the First World War. Since 1918, weaponry has developed even more destructive power, and industry is capable of producing these armaments on an even greater scale. Twenty-first century conflict landscapes may seem far removed from those of the Western Front, but the human experience of modern conflict necessarily entails an assault on the senses. The 2001 World Trade Centre attacks, the 2004 train bombings in Madrid, the 2005 atrocities on London public transport, and the 2015 violence in Paris all show that in modern warfare battle-zones are no longer precisely definable or identifiable – as likely to exist in a Middle Eastern desert as on a bus in a European city. The West is currently involved in a never-ending war on terror, and the propagation of fear by both combatants and governments is changing the sensorial experience of everyday life and society. In this sort of environment odours, sights and sounds take on different and often sinister meanings. Cultural practices, the smell of foreign food and the increasing ubiquity of religious garments all dramatically affect the corporeal ways of engaging with Western society and ideas of conflict. Yet in 1914 many shared a similar experience, as previous concepts of warfare were destroyed and rebuilt, thrusting many different nations together onto (and into) a battle-zone they did not understand.

Archaeology is essential to 'unearthing' the twentieth century's conflict landscapes, and anthropology is the key to understanding how human emotion, experiences and relationships are objectified in them, and how social ideologies and practices can be conveyed through their sensory values.[18] In little over a decade, an anthropology and archaeology of the senses (as an integral part of modern conflict archaeology) has highlighted the potential of interdisciplinary approaches to radically alter how First World War archaeology should be conceived and undertaken. In the research of the underground worlds of the Western Front this need for an inter-disciplinary approach must be recognised, or as archaeologists, we will be left on our own, digging in the dark.

Endnotes

Introduction

1. (Gygi 2004: 75)
2. (See Das 2008: 35-72)
3. (See Saunders 2010: 4-7)
4. The depth of subterranean systems depended on many different factors including geology, the depth of the enemy systems and the time and manpower available to construct the tunnels. At the Butte de Vauquois near Verdun the Germans dug over 100 m (328 ft) beneath the surface in order to get beneath the French fighting tunnels.
5. (Fussell 2000: 44)
6. See Grieve and Newman 1936; Robinson and Cave 2011; Jones 2010; Barrie 1981; Barton et al 2010, Finlayson 2010; Mangold and Penycate 2005.
7. The Durand Group is a fraternal association of like-minded individuals dedicated to the research of military related subterranean features. The Group consists of an eclectic mix of individuals including current and ex-service members, engineers, historians, archaeologists and academics. I have been a member of the Group since 2011 and I currently hold the post of Honourable Secretary. More information on the Group can be found at www.durandgroup.org.uk

Chapter 1

1. (Yadin 1963: 317)
2. (Fuller 1960: 200-219)
3. (Wiggins 2003: 10-11)
4. (Robinson and Cave 2011: 1)
5. (Wiggins 2003: 18-19)
6. (Jones 2010: 14)
7. (Jones 2010: 14)
8. (Jones 2010: 14 – 15)
9. (Jones 2010: 16)

10. (Robinson and Cave 2011: 1)

11. (Westwood 1986: 98)

12. (Costello 1982: 183)

13. (Cooper 2007: 22)

14. (Beevor 2012: 701)

15. (Beevor 2012: 699)

16. (Wright 2005: 139)

17. (See Leckie 1996)

18. (See Leckie 1996)

19. (Mangold and Penycate 2005: 35)

20. (Mangold and Penycate 2005: 67)

21. (Mangold and Penycate 2005: 36)

22. (Mangold and Penycate 2005: 106)

23. (Taylor 2009: 302)

24. (Hecht 2014: 4)

25. (Hecht 2014: 10)

26. (Wright 2007: 229)

27. Lt Col A J Turner. Pers comm., February 2015

28. (See Jones 2010: 29; Robinson and Cave 2011: 2)

29. (Jones 2010: 29)

30. (Grieve and Newman 1936: 26; Barrie 1981: 24)

31. (Grieve and Newman 1936: 25)

32. (Grieve and Newman 1936: 30 – 31)

33. Throughout the war the Germans remained the masters of the mine crater. They had an uncanny knack of being first to the crater lips and the British and the French struggled to gain the upper hand. At Messines in 1917, the British did manage to ain control of the craters, but this was largely because the Germans troops, packed into the frontline positions to defend against an expected attack, were destroyed almost entirely by the nineteen mines detonated at the start of the battle.

34. (Fussell 2000: 41)

35. (Fussell 2000: 44)

36. (Fussell 2000: 41)

37. (Robinson and Cave 2011: 4)

38. (Robinson and Cave 2011: 4)

39. (Robinson and Cave 2011: 6)

40. The largest mine of the war was blown by the Germans at the Butte de Vauquois on 14 May 1916. Some 60 tonnes of explosive was detonated creating a crater 60m in diameter).

41. See Glossary

42. As all the Canadian 'attestation papers' (forms signed by men when they joined up) are available online, the past and present can be linked through soldiers' graffiti, revealing important details about individual soldier's war experiences.

43. (Quoted in Keegan 1999: 354)

Chapter 2

1.   (Terraine 1982: 144)

2.   (Carrington, Quoted in Leed 2009: 14)

3.   (Dyer 2009: 120)

4.   (Barbusse 2003: 139)

5.   (Hynes 1992: 189-202)

6.   (Classen 1997: 401)

7.   (Marinetti 2005: 331)

8.   (Sacks 2005: 28)

9.   (Zajonic 1995: 2)

10. (Hurcombe 2007: 539)

11. (Descartes, quoted in Ingold 2000: 253)

12. (Ingold 2000: 255)

13. (Saunders 2009: 27-40)

14. (Briffault. Quoted in Cecil 1997: 430)

15. (Owen, Quoted in Das 2008: 8)

16. (Stewart 2005: 62)

17. (An unnamed German soldier, Quoted in Leed 2009: 140)

18. (Classen 2005: 148-152)

19. (Popenoe 2004: 172)

20. (See Edensor 2007)

21. (See Laviolette 2009)

22. (See Burchell 2014)

23. (Paterson 2007: 81-82)

24. (Das 2008: 188-197)
25. (Das 2008: 111)
26. (Das 2008: 116)
27. (See Corbin 1998)
28. (Saunders 2010: 68)
29. (See Leed 2009)
30. (See Basso 1996)
31. (Classen 2005b: 153-157)
32. (Saunders 2001: 220-236)
33. (Imal 2006)
34. (See Law 2005)
35. (Smith 2007: 79-80)
36. (Robinson and Cave 2011: 9)
37. (Füsslein, Quoted in Barton et al 2010: 98)
38. (Westacott, Quoted in Barton et al 2010: 137)
39. (Grieve and Newman 1936: 311-315)
40. (Robinson and Cave 2011: 2-3)
41. (Barton et al 2010: 144)
42. (Marx, Quoted in Howes 2003: 206)
43. (McIvor and Johnston 2007: 30)
44. (Fussell 2000: 41)
45. (Robinson and Cave 2011: 4)
46. (McIvor and Johnston 2007: 50) & P. Robinson 2013, pers. comm., May

Chapter 3
1. (Stichelbaut, B. Bourgeois, J. Saunders, N & Chielens, P. (eds.) 2009)
2. (Duffett 2012)
3. (Saunders 2013; Leonard 2015)
4. (Adie 2013)
5. (Saunders 2003)
6. (Carden-Coyne 2009)
7. (See Das 2008; Fussell 2000)
8. (Dendooven and Chielens 2008)
9. (Keegan 2004: 231)

10. (Keegan 1999: 385)
11. For a thorough explanation of how the battlefields were reclaimed after 1918 see Clout, H. (1996). *After The Ruins: Restoring the Countryside of Northern France after the Great War.* Exeter: Exeter University Press.
12. In preparation for the battle the British tunnelling companies had laid twenty-five mines. One was cut off by the detonation of a German camouflet charge and another by a tunnel collapse. Four at the southern end of the Ridge were deemed tactically unnecessary, and it was one of these that exploded in 1955.
13. See Glossary
14. See Glossary
15. The Group's work underground has been published by various members across a wide range of commercially produced literature. Three Group members have also used the underground war and the Durand Group's work as a primary source for two Bachelor of Arts dissertations, one Masters degree and a PhD thesis.

Chapter 4
1. (Keegan 1999: 219)
2. (Keegan 1999: 219)
3. (Rawson 2003: 25)
4. (Rawson 2002: 47)
5. (Rawson 2002: 54)
6. At this early stage of the war the British were woefully short of heavy artillery and shells. The production of war material was still in its infancy and although this situation was rectified by the middle of the following year, at Loos the lack of artillery support was a major factor in the high casualty figures. Many German machine gun nests and artillery positions were left in tact, and the British were unable to shell the German reserve lines to the required extent, meaning any gaps in the their lines to be constantly plugged.
7. (Smith 2007: 80)
8. (Rawson 2002: 40)
9. (Rawson 2002: 40)
10. (Rawson 2003: 21)
11. (Grieve and Newman 1936: 192)
12. (Leed 2009: 147)
13. (Grieve and Newman 1936: 191-192)

14.   (Leed 2009: 147; Grieve and Newman 1936: 195)

15.   (Grieve and Newman 1936: 194)

16.   (Rawson 2003: 134)

17.   (Coppard 1999: 34-35)

18.   (Charles Bean, Australian Official Historian of the Great War)

19.   (Finlayson 2010: 179)

20.   (173 Tunnelling Company War Diary, 13 January 1916)

21.   (Pers. comm. A Prada 2015 – Project manager of the Durand Group project 'Engineering the Loos Salient 2015-2018'. Further details of this long running project will be forthcoming in Prada, A (In Press). *Blood, Rust and Chalk: Uncovering the Loos Salient*. Barnsley. Pen and Sword.)

22.   (Finlayson 2010: 7)

23.   (Finlayson 2010: 179)

24.   (3rd Australian Tunnelling Company War Diary 1917: 4)

25.   (3rd Australian Tunnelling Company War Diary 1917: 6)

26.   (3rd Australian Tunnelling Company War Diary 1917: 8)

27.   (Sanderson 2012: 10-12)

28.   See Glossary

29.   (Grieve and Newman 1936: 39)

30.   (Grieve and Newman 1936: 47)

31.   (Barrie 1981: 145)

32.   (Grieve and Newman 1936: 95)

33.   (Barrie 1981: 145)

34.   At the end of 1914 underground war had not yet become a serious undertaking on any side. Nevertheless, at Loos there were several shallow tunnels (mainly covered trenches known as Russian Saps. Also see Glossary), dugouts and tentative fighting systems by the end of the year.

35.   (Balbi 2009: 280 – 290)

36.   (Barrie 1981: 207) – Tar papering and wood panelling improved the aesthetics of dugouts, and panelling, timber, and metal was used when possible to shore up walls and ceilings. Different nations also approached the construction of the underground according to more ephemeral criteria. Europeans, Maori, and the descendents of First Nation Canadians are just some of the diverse cultures that worked beneath the Western Front. Their different approaches to tradition, religion, taboo and ways of engaging with the landscape all left their imprint on the subterranean battlefield. (See also Leonard (2016 – In Press). Assaulting the senses:

life and landscape beneath the Western Front. In N, J, Saunders and P, Cornish. (eds). *Killer Instincts?: Modern conflict and the senses*. London: Routledge)

Chapter 5

1.   (See Robinson and Cave 2011; Sheldon 2008; Cave 2014)

2.   (Robinson and Cave 2011: 14)

3.   (Robinson and Cave 2011: 15)

4.   (Barrie 1981: 174)

5.   (Barbusse 2003: 139)

6.   (Barbusse 2003: 141)

7.   (Plummer, Quoted in Robinson and Cave 2011: 131)

8.   (Barrie 1981: 175)

9.   (Grieve and Newman 1936: 141)

10.   (Grieve and Newman 1936: 142)

11.   (Grieve and Newman 1936: 141)

12.   (Robinson and Cave 2011: 92)

13.   (Robinson and Cave 2011: 27)

14.   (Robinson and Cave 2011: 27; Keegan 1999: 215-216; Cave 2009: 23-26)

15.   (Robinson and Cave 2011: 27)

16.   (Robinson and Cave 2011: 27, Grieve and Newman 1936: 157)

17.   (Robinson and Cave 2011: 29-30)

18.   (Williamson 2009: 116-117)

19.   (Williamson 2009: 117)

20.   (Williamson 2009: 117)

21.   (See Becker 1999; Decock 1996; Hawkins 2012)

22.   (Becker 1999: 126)

23.   (91st Battalion War Diary, Feb 1918: 8)

24.   (Williamson 2009: 116-117)

25.   (History of the 15th Battalion CEF (48th Highlanders of Canada), Quoted in Robinson and Cave 2011: 27)

26.   On 9 April 1917 there were twelve subways in existence beneath the Vimy Ridge. However, if the Pylonnes subway is considered to be a single entity and not part of Goodman, then the number should be thirteen. There was also the rather obscure 'No 33 subway' and if this minor tunnel is included then the number is fourteen. Finally, on 12 April 1917 the Canadian

4th Division added the Souchez Subway. There were also a number of subways on the XVII Corps front, but none were as extensive as those on the northern half of the Ridge.

27. It should be noted that the subways remained in use after the initial assault, and some of the graffiti recorded in the Goodman Subway is dated 1918. However, they were never again used for their prime purpose after 8/9 April 1917.

28. It should also be noted that locals removed anything that could be useful for temporary shelters and the reconstruction of their shattered livelihoods. Recycling war material like this was common practice across the Western Front and continued long after the war, arguably to some degree even up to the present day.

29. (Chalmers 1998: 7-19)

30. Some of the subways had extensive provision for accommodation, notably the Cavalier and Tottenham subways in the 4th Cdn Division area.

31. (Robinson and Cave 2011: 227)

32. The sanitary conditions in the Grange warrant some clarification. There are no specific records of the exact deprivations suffered in the Grange between 7-9 April 1917, but it is not hard to imagine. These sorts of details are often absent from diaries and records, and a hygiene team was allocated to Grange. If at all possible buckets would have been emptied on the surface, but that would have been no easy task. Even modern sanitation would struggle to deal with the demands of so many people in such a cramped environment at such a traumatic time.

33. (See Dendooven 2013)

34. (Barbusse 2003: 7)

35. (Blunden 2009: 160)

36. (Cave 2009: 125)

37. See Glossary

38. P. Robinson 2014, pers. comm., January

Chapter 6

1. (Keegan 2004: 210)

2. (Horne 1993: 1)

3. (Leed 2009: 104)

4. (Blunden 2000: 98)

5. (Horne 1993: 45; Ousby 2003: 51; Terraine 1982: 227)

6. (Horne 1993: 45)

7.   (Horne 1993: 55)

8.   (Horne 1993: 58)

9.   (Horne 1993: 105)

10. (Terraine 1982: 218)

11. (Holstein 2009: 9)

12. (Holstein 2009: 10)

13. The Dreyfus Affair was a scandal that tore through France in the late 19th and early 20th centuries. Alfred Dreyfus was a Jewish artillery captain in the French army, who was tried and convicted for revealing military secrets to the Germans. It was the result of a torn-up letter found in a bin at the German Embassy in Paris in 1894. Dreyfus was convicted on the spurious evidence that the note was in his handwriting, and he was ordered to complete his sentence on the notorious Devil's Island. He also suffered the indignity of being paraded through Paris, the insignia of rank torn from his uniform, while people yelled at him, calling him a traitor. In 1896, Georges Picquart, the Army's new head, found evidence that suggesting another French officer, Major Ferdinand Esterhazy, was the real traitor. Picquart was discouraged from continuing his investigation by the military and political hierarchy and then was promptly transferred to North Africa and later imprisoned. The secret was soon out and in 1898 Esterhazy was court-martialed. Incredibly, he was found not guilty. After the trial an open letter 'J'Accuse…!', penned by Emile Zola, was printed in the press accusing the military of dishonesty. Zola was charged with libel. In 1899, Dreyfus was court-martialed again, and again found guilty. It was a sham and Dreyfus was pardoned shortly afterwards by the French president, although it took until 1906 for Dreyfus to be cleared and allowed to rejoin the army. The affair was a great embarrassment to the establishment and to the army. It highlighted all that was wrong with the military, and this formed a convenient excuse for why France had been so utterly defeated in the Franco-Prussian War.

14. (Horne 1993: 12)

15. (Horne 1993: 12)

16. (Ousby 2003: 51)

17. (Jones 2010: 58-59)

18. (Saunders 2004: 5)

19. (Jones 2010: 60)

20. (Jones 2010: 61)

21. (Romains 1973: 88-89)

22. (Romains 1973: 88-89)

23. (Romains 1973: 86)

24. (Jones 2010: P 63)

25. (Jones 2010: 63)

26. (Smith 2007: 9)

27. (Smith 2007: 82)

28. (Smith 2007: 78)

29. (Alighieri 2011: 32 Kindle Edition)

30. (Ousby 2003: 9)

31. (Jones 2010: 63)

32. (Romains 1973: 92)

33. (Summer 2012: 61)

34. (Jones 2010: 73)

35. (Summer 2012: 61)

36. (Horne 1993: 106)

37. (Horne 1993: 106)

38. (Horne 1993: 105-109)

39. (Horne 1993: 112)

40. (Horne 1993: 116)

41. (Horne 1993: 252)

42. (Horne 1993: 252-253)

43. (Horne 1993: 255)

44. (Horne 1993: 257)

45. (Horne 1993: 259)

46. (Ousby 2003: 218; Horne 1993: 261)

47. (Horne1993: 263)

48. (Horne1993: 263)

49. (Horne1993: 264)

50. (Ousby 2003: 214)

51. (Ousby 2003: 214)

52. (Ousby 2003: 251)

53. (Ousby 2003: 251)

54. The Voie Sacrée was the name given to the only serviceable French supply route to Verdun. It was essential to the French and great care was kept to keep it open at all costs. During the week beginning 28 February 1916

more than 190,000 men and 25,000 tonnes of supplies were transported along its length. The volume of traffic peaked in June 1916 when a vehicle passed along it every 14 seconds.

55. (Terraine 1982: 209)
56. (Horne 1993: 268)
57. (Horne 1993: 268)
58. (Winter 2009: 99)
59. (Holstien 2009: 141)
60. Horne 1993: 268
61. (Horne 1993: 268-269; Ousby 2003: 267)
62. (Winter 2009: 102)
63. (Horne 1993: 326-327)
64. (Horne 1993: 301)
65. (Ousby 2003: 265)
66. (Leed 2009: 104)
67. (Saunders 2010: 97)
68. (Holstein 2009: 147)
69. (Holstein 2009: 147)
70. (Arthur: 2003: 144)
71. (Ousby 2003: 5-6)

Chapter 7

1. (Keegan 1999: 109)
2. (Terraine 1982: 90)
3. (Keegan 1999: 109)
4. (See Barbusse 2003; Blunden 2009; Jünger 2004; Sassoon 1997)
5. (See Das 2008; Fussell 2000; Leed 2009; Saunders 2010)
6. (Howes and Classen 2014: 1)
7. In the Westernised world we navigate our environments predominantly using our eyes. Visual aesthetic, signage and the ability to read all govern how we conduct our lives. In many other parts of the world this is not the case. The eyes are obviously still used, but the power of the other senses often carries more importance culturally.
8. Night-time trench raids were a hated part of life. In an enemy trench in the middle of the night a silent and easily usable weapon was often preferred to the cumbersome rifle. This gave rise to many inventive hand held

weapons. Modern equipment was regularly eschewed in favour of my archaic instruments. Barbusse refers (Le Feu) to a soldier finding a stone-age axe head while digging a trench, who uses it as a trench club due to its enduring efficiency.

9.   (Ninh 1998: 2-3)
10.   (Homer 2008: 214)
11.   (Das 2008: 43)
12.   (Das 2008: 35)
13.   (e.g. Clark: 1991)
14.   (See Robinson and Cave 2011; Cave 2009)
15.   (Ingold 2011: 47)
16.   (Ingold 2004: 330)
17.   (Howes and Classen 2014: 73)
18.   (Howes 2005: 4)

Bibliography

Alighieri, D. (2011). *The Divine Comedy*. Public Domain.

Adie, K. (2013). *Fighting on the Home Front: The Legacy of Women in World War One.* London: Hodder & Stoughton.

Arthur, M. (2003). *Forgotten Voices of the Great War*. London: Ebury Press.

Balbi, M. (2009). Great War Archaeology on the Glaciers of the Alps. In, N. J. Saunders and P. Cornish. (eds.). *Contested Objects: Material Memories of the Great War,* pp 280 – 290. Abingdon: Routledge.

Barbusse, H. (2003). *Under Fire*. London: Penguin Books.

Barrie, A. (1981). *War Underground*. London: Star Books.

Barton, P, Doyle, P and Vandewalle, J. (2010). *Beneath Flanders Fields. The Tunellers' War 1914-1918*. Stroud: Spellmount.

Basso, K, H. (1996). *Wisdom Sits in Places*. Albuquerque: University of New Mexico Press.

Becker, A. (1999). 'Graffiti et Sculptures de Soldats'. *L'Archéologie et la Grande Guerre Aujourd'hui. Noesis: Revue Annuelle d'Histoire,* 2, pp 117-127.

Beevor, A. (2012). *The Second World War*. London: Weidenfeld and Nicolson.

Blunden, E. (2009). *Undertones of War.* London: Penguin Classics.

Burchell, M. (2014). Skilful Movements: The Evolving Commando. In N. J. Saunders and P. Cornish. (eds.). *Bodies in Conflict: Corporeality, Materiality and Transformation*, pp 208-218. Abingdon: Routledge.

Carden-Coyne, A. (2009). *Reconstructing the Body: Classicism, Modernism, and the First World War.* Oxford: Oxford University Press.

Cave, N. (2009). *Vimy Ridge*. Barnsley: Pen and Sword.

Cecil, H. (1997). Passchendaele – A selection of British and German War Veteran Literature. In P. Liddle. (ed.). *Passchendaele In Perspective: The Third Battle of Ypres*, pp 422-436. London: Pen and Sword Books Ltd.

Chalmers, D. (1998). The Extended Mind. ANALYSIS 58: 1: pp.7-19

Clark, A. (1991). *The Donkeys*. London: Pimlico.

Classen, C. (1997). Foundations for an anthropology of the senses. *International Social Science Journal,* 49: 401–412.

--- (2005). McLuhan in the Rainforest: The Sensory Worlds of Oral Cultures. In D. Howes. (ed.). *Empire Of The Senses,* pp 147-163. New York: Berg.

Cooper, L. (2007). *The War in the Pacific – A Retrospective.* Malibu: 90 Day Wonder Publishing.

Corbin, A. (1998). *Village Bells: Sound and Meaning in the 19th century French Countryside*. New York: Columbia University Press.

Costello, J. (1982). *The Pacific War 1941 – 1945*. New York: Perennial

Das, S. (2008). *Touch and Intimacy in First World War Literature.* New York: Cambridge University Press.

Decock, B. (1996). 'L'Art rupestre des soldats de la Grande Guerre: La Carriere du "Premier Zouaves" de Confrécourt', *Guerres mondiales et conflits contemporains*, 46 Number 183: pp 141-9.

Dendooven, D. (2013). *Trench Crap: Excremental aspects of the First World War.* In *Conflict and the Senses: Materialities and Cultural Memory of 20th Century Conflict conference*, September 6-7, 2013. London: Imperial War Museum.

--- and Chielens, P. (2008). *World War One: Five Continents in Flanders*. Tielt: Lannoo.

Duffett, R. (2012). *The Stomach for Fighting: Food and the Soldiers of the Great War.* Manchester: Manchester University Press.

Dyer, G. (2009). *The Missing of the Somme*. London: Phoenix.

Edensor, T. (2007). Sensing the Ruin. *Sense and Society*. 2 (2): 217-232.

Finlayson, D. (2010). *Crumps and Camouflets. Australian Tunnelling Companies on the Western Front*. Newport: Big Sky Publishing.

Fuller, J, F, C. (1960). *The Generalship of Alexander the Great*. New Jersey: Da Capo.

Fussell, P. (2000). *The Great War and Modern Memory*. New York: Oxford University Press.

Grieve, W, G (Capt) and Newman, B. (1936). *Tunnellers: The Story of the Tunnelling Companies, Royal Engineers, during the World War*. London: Herbert Jenkins Limited.

Gygi, F. (2004). Shattered Experiences – Recycled Relics: Strategies of representation and the legacy of the Great War. In N. J. Saunders. (ed.). *Matters of Conflict. Material culture, memory and the First World War,* pp. 72-89. Abingdon: Routledge.

Hecht, E. (2015). *The Tunnels in Gaza*. Testimony before the UN Commission of Inquiry on the 2014 Gaza Conflict. February 2015.

Holstein, C. (2009). *Walking Verdun*. Barnsley: Pen and Sword.

Homer. (2008). *The Iliad*. Oxford: Oxford University Press. (Translation by R. Fitzgerald.)

Horne, A. (1993). *The price of Glory: Verdun 1916*. London: Penguin.

Howes, D. (2003). *Sensual Relations: Engaging the Senses in Culture and Social Theory*. Ann Arbor: University of Michigan Press.

--- (2005). Introduction. In D. Howes. (ed.). *Empire Of The Senses,* pp 1-17. New York: Berg.

--- and Classen, C. (2014). *Ways of Sensing: Understanding the Senses in Society*. London: Routledge.

Hurcombe, L. (2007). A sense of materials and sensory perception in concepts of materiality. *World Archaeology*, 39 (4), pp 532-545.

Hynes, S. (1992). *A War Imagined – The First World War and English Literature*. London: Pimlico.

Imal, H. (2006). Senses on the Move: Multisensory Encounters with Street Vendors in the Japanese Urban Alleyway *Roji. Sense and Society. Vol. 3, Issue 3,* pp 329-338.

Ingold, T. (2000). *The Perception of the Environment: Essays on Livelihood, dwelling and Skill*. London: Routledge.

--- (2004). Culture on the Ground. *Journal of Material Culture* Vol. 9 (3), pp 315-340.

--- (2011). *Being Alive: Essays on Movement, Knowledge and Description*. Abingdon: Routledge.

Jones, S. (2010). *Underground Warfare 1914-1918*. Barnsley: Pen and Sword.

Keegan, J. (1999). *The First World War*. London: Pimlico.

--- (2004). *The Face of Battle*. London: Pimlico.

Laviolette, P. (2009). Fearless Trembling: A Leap of Faith into the Devil's Frying Pan. *Sense and Society*. Vol. 4 (3), pp 303-322.

Law, L. (2005). Home Cooking: Filipino Women and the Geographies of the Senses in Hong Kong. In D. Howes. (ed.). *Empire Of The Senses,* pp 224-244. New York: Berg.

Leckie, R. ((2011). *Helmet for my Pillow*. Reading: Random House.

Leed, E, J. (2009). *No Man's Land: Combat and Identity in World War One*. New York: Cambridge University Press.

Leonard, M. (2015). *Poppyganda*. Eastbourne: Uniform Press.

Mangold, T and Penycate, J. (2005). *The Tunnels of Cu Chi: A Remarkable Story of War in Vietnam*. London: Cassell.

Marinetti, F, T. (2005), Tactilism. In C. Classen. (ed.). *The Book of Touch*, pp 329-332. Oxford: Berg.

McIvor, A and Johnston R. (2007). *Miner's Lung: A History of Dust Disease in British Coal Mining*. Aldershot: Ashgate Publishing Limited.

Ninh, B. (1988). *The Sorrow of War*. London: Vintage.

Ousby, I. (2003). *The Road To Verdun*. London. Pimlico.

Paterson, M. (2007). *The Senses of Touch. Haptics, Affects and Technologies*. Oxford: Berg.

Popenoe, R. (2004). *Feeding Desire: Fatness, Beauty and Sexuality among a Saharan People*. London: Routledge.

Rawson, A. (2002). *Loos – Hill 70*. Barnsley: Pen and Sword.

--- (2003). *Loos – Hohenzollern*, Barnsley: Pen and Sword.

Robinson, P and Cave, N. (2011). *The Underground War: Vimy Ridge to Arras*. Barnsley: Pen and Sword.

Romains, J. (1973). *Verdun*. St Albans: Mayflower Books.

Sacks, O. (2005). The Mind's Eye, What Blind People See. In D. Howes. (ed.). *Empire Of The Senses*, pp 25-42. New York: Berg.

Sanderson, R. (2012). Digging Deep in the Tunnels of Time. *In Trust News Australia*. Vol 5, No 8, pp 10-12.

Saunders, N, J. (2001). A Dark Light: Reflections on Obsidian in Mesoamerica. *World Archaeology, Vol. 33, No. 2, Archaeology and Aesthetics,* pp. 220-236.

--- (2003). *Trench Art: Materialities and Memories of War*. Oxford: Berg.

--- (2004). (ed.). *Matters of Conflict. Material culture, memory and the First World War,* Abingdon: Routledge.

--- (2010). *Killing Time. Archaeology and the First World War*. Stroud: The History Press.

--- (2013). *The Poppy: A Cultural History from Ancient Egypt to Flanders Fields to Afghanistan*. London: Oneworld.

Saunders, N. J. and Cornish, P. (2009). Introduction: Contested Objects, Material Memories of The Great War. In N. J. Saunders and P. Cornish. (eds.). , pp. 1-10. Abingdon: Routledge.

--- (2014) (eds.). *Bodies in Conflict: Corporeality, Materiality and Transformation*. Abingdon: Routledge.

Smith, L, V. (2007). *The Embattled Self. French Soldiers' Testimony of the Great War*. New York: Cornell University Press.

Stewart, S. (2005). Remembering The Senses. In D. Howes. (ed.). *Empire Of The Senses*, pp 59-69. New York: Berg.

Stichelbaut, B. Bourgeois, J. Saunders, N. & Chielens, P. (eds.). *Images of Conflict: Military Aerial Photography and Archaeology*. Newcastle Upon Tyne: Cambridge Scholars Publishing.

Summer, I. (2012). *They Shall Not Pass: The French Army on the Western Front 1914-1918*. Barnsley: Pen and Sword.

Taylor, F, (2009). *The Berlin Wall: 13 August 1961– 9 November 1989*. London: Bloomsbury.

Terraine, J. (1982). *White Heat: The New Warfare 1914-18*. London: Book Club Associates.

Westwood, J, N. (1986). *Russia Against Japan, 1904-1905: A New Look at the Russo-Japanese war*. Albany: State University of New York Press.

Wiggins, K. (2003). *Siege Mines and Underground Warfare*. Princess Risborough: Shire.

Williamson, H. (2009). *The Wet Flanders Plain*. London: Faber and Faber.

Winter, J. (2009). *Sites of Memory, Sites of Mourning: The Great War in European Cultural History*. New York: Cambridge University Press.

Wright, D. (2005). *To the Far Side of Hell: The Battle of Peleliu, 1944*. Marlborough: The Crowood Press.

Wright, L. (2007). *The Looming Tower: Al Qaeda's Road to 9/11*. New York: Penguin

Yadin, Y. (1963). *The Art of Warfare in Biblical Lands, Volume 1*. New York: McGraw-Hill Book Company.

Zajonic, A. (1995). *Catching the Light: The Entwined History of Light and Mind*. Oxford: Oxford University Press.

Index